"Our churches desperately need to move beyond the spiritual infancy of merely wading in the shallows and begin to plunge with determined dedication into spiritual ocean depths. Spiritual formation has emerged as a great need of the hour, but biblically grounded, Christ-focused spiritual formation is paramount. Graham Joseph Hill has expertly crafted such a resource to assist in meeting this great need. May it be warmly embraced and bear much fruit."

—Paul Quicke
Lead pastor, Morley Baptist Church

"I always walked into Graham Joseph Hill's seminary classes with a heart full of expectation. Now, opening his books evokes that same excitement. This new devotion is a deep river of spiritual insight. Dive in and be refreshed."

—Tim Kay
Senior pastor, Thornleigh Community Baptist Church

"It is with great joy that I offer my wholehearted endorsement for this daily devotional. Graham Joseph Hill's deeply insightful reflections take the profound truths of Scripture and present them in a wonderfully helpful, accessible form. This inspiring devotional work is a blessing, and I look forward to the subsequent volumes."

—Nick Scott
Senior pastor, Mount Pleasant Baptist Church

"This devotional is for you if you want a concise, thoughtful engagement with the Bible. Graham Joseph Hill's deep theological reflections challenge the reader to consider how this book of the Bible impacts us today. I have found this to be an excellent yet challenging companion in my daily reflection time."

—Sally Pim
Intercultural team member, Mozambique, Baptist Mission Australia

"Graham Joseph Hill's book of devotionals is a refreshing well of rediscovery into the Bible. No topic is overlooked here; from the depth of sin to the absurdity of God's grace freely given, serious treatment has been given to the overarching themes of the Christian faith. This is a stellar contribution to what will no doubt be a series of devotionals that will impact a generation of believers with the awe, hope, and promise of God and his word."

—Ed Divine
Team leader, Quinns Baptist Church

"In a world of potential distractions, Graham Joseph Hill skillfully and sensitively encourages us to draw near to God so that we too might hear the heartbeat of the living God speaking through Scripture in the context of God's redemptive story. Hill's devotions are profoundly beautiful to read, deeply encouraging, and sufficiently challenging in application and as a teaching resource for a broad spectrum of people, whether they be an inquirer or a seasoned disciple."

—Ann Clews
Follower of Jesus Christ

Matthew

Daily Devotions with Jesus

Matthew

Seeking the Kingdom and Pursuing Righteousness:
A Fifty-Day Devotional

GRAHAM JOSEPH HILL

WIPF & STOCK · Eugene, Oregon

MATTHEW
Seeking the Kingdom and Pursuing Righteousness: A Fifty-Day Devotional

Wipf & Stock
An Imprint of Wipf and Stock Publishers
199 W. 8th Ave., Suite 3
Eugene, OR 97401

www.wipfandstock.com

PAPERBACK ISBN: 979-8-3852-1157-9
HARDCOVER ISBN: 979-8-3852-1158-6
EBOOK ISBN: 979-8-3852-1159-3

VERSION NUMBER 020824

For my daughter, Grace,
whose love for God and people
points hearts toward Jesus, "God with us."

Contents

Contents

CONTENTS

Contents

Introduction

IN THE DAILY DEVOTIONS with Jesus series, Rev. Dr. Graham Joseph Hill guides you through the entire Bible, moving from Genesis to Revelation. Daily Devotions with Jesus podcasts and devotional books show you how each book of the Bible can shape your spiritual life and actions in the world. This is a groundbreaking Bible podcast and devotional book series. See how each book of the Bible deepens your faith and inspires you to follow Jesus in life-changing ways!

The Gospel of Matthew is a spiritual bridge between the Old and New Testaments, capturing the essence of Jesus Christ's life, teachings, and profound impact on humanity. This Gospel is often hailed as the "teaching Gospel," rich in parables, discourses, and instructive events that guide us in our spiritual walk. From the Sermon on the Mount to the Great Commission, Matthew lays a foundational framework for living a life that's not just religious but deeply spiritual.

The narrative begins with a genealogy that connects Jesus to the lineage of David and Abraham, establishing him as the long-awaited Messiah. What follows are stories of miraculous healings, the casting out of demons, and interactions that reveal the heart of God—compassionate, just, and infinitely wise. Matthew records vital teachings like the Beatitudes, overturning worldly values to highlight the spiritual virtues that genuinely matter. Phrases like "Blessed are the meek, for they shall inherit the earth" encourage us to see life from a different vantage point, focusing on eternal significance rather than temporal success.

In a world that often seems chaotic, the Gospel of Matthew teaches us about the kingdom of heaven—a kingdom not of this world but one that we can bring into our daily lives. Jesus instructs us to seek first this heavenly kingdom and its righteousness. The Gospel calls us to a deeper relationship with God, encouraging us to forgive as we have been forgiven, to love our neighbors as ourselves, and to lead lives of humble service. By applying the teachings found in Matthew, we enrich our spiritual lives, align ourselves more closely with God's will, and better understand our role as ambassadors of God's kingdom on earth.

Dive deep into Matthew, the first book of the New Testament. This Gospel invites us into a loving, transformative relationship with Jesus Christ. Through a dedicated fifty-day journey, readers will explore Matthew, unveiling its broader significance within the tapestry of Scripture.

Rooted in rigorous biblical and theological scholarship, this devotional encourages a fuller understanding of the Gospel of Matthew and its relevance in today's world. Each day, readers are invited to meditate on a passage, reflecting on its overarching themes and intricate details. This holistic approach illuminates vital messages often overlooked in cursory or superficial readings.

This daily devotional doesn't shy away from biblical and theological depth. It makes no apology for pushing you to dive deeply into the theological and biblical meanings of the chapters you read. However, this journey isn't merely intellectual. It beckons the heart and spirit, urging readers to engage in intimate conversations with God, share the timeless message of the gospel, and be invigorated toward Christ-glorifying action. Drawing from the ancient narratives, readers will find inspiration to advocate for peace, champion justice, foster reconciliation, extend mercy, and actively partake in society's transformation.

Deep immersion in Scripture invariably leads to a more profound understanding of God's word and its implications for our lives. This devotional, rich with thought-provoking questions and guided prayers, catalyzes a deeper relationship with God. As you turn each page, may you be drawn closer to God's heart and spurred on to walk in the footsteps of Jesus. This journey through Matthew is the second book in a series of devotional books designed to guide you through the entire Bible, nourishing your soul, renewing your purpose, and deepening your theology, contemplation, and action.

Here's what is inside this devotional and how best to use it:

1. The devotional covers the entire Gospel of Matthew over fifty days.

2. Use this book with the Daily Devotions with Jesus podcast—https://grahamjosephhill.com/devotions.

3. Every day as you work your way through this devotional:

   a. *Read* the Bible passage slowly and prayerfully.

   b. *Listen* to the podcast episode for this Bible passage.

   c. *Reflect* on the spiritual devotional.

   d. *Pray* over the Bible passage and devotional and their meanings for your life and the world.

   e. *Act* on your insights.

Reading this Matthew devotional alone, with family, or with a group will help you understand the Bible more fully and put it into practice. Get ready to change.

All Scripture quotations, unless otherwise indicated, are taken from the World English Bible.

Day 1

The Mosaic of Divine Inclusion

Reading: Matthew 1:1-17

Matthew 1 invites us into the intricate mosaic of human lineage, pieced together with divine intention, as we read the genealogy of Jesus. At first glance, one might rush through this litany of names, but to do so would be to gloss over the profound. The list is more than a historical record; it affirms that God is involved in humanity's messy, painful, complicated, and beautiful family lines and stories. Tamar, Rahab, and Ruth—women of foreign origin—are named and honored here. The Christ emerges not from a sanitized lineage but one crammed with real stories of human frailty and faithlessness, stories of lives celebrated and marginalized, both noble and ordinary people. There are stories of brokenness and courage—God at work in both expected and surprising places through grace, providence, and love.

This genealogy is about Jesus—a lineage that helps establish him as Jesus the Messiah. Yet, this chapter also speaks volumes about God's acceptance and grace. The genealogy reminds us that no one is beyond the reach of divine love. If God can work through a lineage replete with brokenness, Jesus Christ can work through us. This speaks to the heart of humility—our awareness that we're not the sum of our virtues or vices. God holds us within a greater story that both dignifies and humbles us.

How does this inform the way we live as Jesus's disciples? If God is willing to fully enter the human condition through a lineage marked by both saints and sinners, what is our excuse for withholding mercy, love, or justice from others? We find here a charge to radical inclusivity, echoing the reconciling work of Jesus. And it's not just about people; it extends to all creation. In Jesus, God says, "Behold, I make all things new" (Rev 21: 5). Our call, then, is to join this great work of cosmic renovation with care for the earth, advocacy for the marginalized, and a pursuit of justice and peace that leaves no one behind.

Jesus gives us a ministry of reconciliation and inclusion— tearing down walls that divide us and showing by our actions that no one is too broken or flawed to be outside God's love and purpose.

Big Idea: Embrace your place of belonging in God's intricate mosaic of grace, as it calls you to radical inclusivity, mercy, and love.

Reflection: How does your life reflect God's inclusive, merciful heart? How can you participate in God's work of making "all things new"?

Prayer: God of Abraham, Isaac, Jacob, and all peoples, you are also the God of our stories and histories. Thank you for grafting us into the tree of your people, flawed yet chosen. Please help us to recognize your image in ourselves and everyone we encounter. May we be ambassadors of your radical love, grace, and justice. Amen.

Day 2

Embodying "God With Us"

Reading: Matthew 1:18–25

This passage beckons us into the astonishing mystery of the incarnation, God becoming fully human in Jesus Christ. Matthew draws our attention to the name "Immanuel," which means "God with us." This name, reverberating from Isaiah 7:14, shatters any notion of an aloof, disinterested deity. God doesn't merely watch or supervise from a lofty vantage point but plunges into the mess, chaos, pain, joy, beauty, and wonder of human existence—every aspect of our lives.

When we think about "Immanuel," it's not just a theological concept but an embodied reality—God engages profoundly in our world's struggles, sorrows, and joys. It means God is passionately interested in the marginalized, the lonely, the grieving, and the oppressed, beckoning us to serve "the least of these" as if we were serving Jesus himself. Just as "God is with us," Jesus calls us to be fully present in a world plagued by absence, isolation, and abandonment. "God with us" is a declaration of love, so Jesus also invites us to lifestyles of loving presence. This passage asks us to be a healing, compassionate, hopeful presence; to offer not just charity but solidarity; not just relief but justice; not only peace but reconciliation; not only our prayers but our presence embodying "God with us."

As you reflect on Matthew 1, allow it to shape your compassionate, courageous presence among your family, church, and world. Let the courage of Joseph fortify your will, the name of Immanuel soften your heart, and the unfolding narrative of salvation widen your vision. Be a vessel of healing presence, pursuing justice and mercy as if God were the recipient. Love fellow believers, strangers, neighbors, and enemies as opportunities to encounter the living God. Be present with the despised and marginalized, as Jesus was, and as a living embodiment of "God with us."

God's presence is often most potent and prophetic among the least and the last, the forgotten and despised, the sinners and "unrighteous." God is with the church, Christ's holy, restored people. But God is also present in the most surprising places. Jesus is frequently "God with us" through the lives of people who are often ignored or shunned: those marginalized because of race, gender, sexual orientation, disability, poverty, religion, and other factors. Immanuel and the kingdom of God are among these.

Big Idea: Embody "God with us" through a compassionate, courageous, and loving presence, especially among the marginalized and in unexpected places.

Reflection: What does "God with us" mean for how you interact with those around you, especially the overlooked and marginalized? How can you emulate Joseph's courageous obedience in the face of social and religious pressures?

Prayer: Immanuel, please make us aware of your vivid presence in our lives and the lives of others. Grant us the courage to subvert the world's expectations, that we may be your hands and feet, your people of healing and reconciliation. Amen.

Day 3

Seeking Jesus Christ in Life's Pilgrimage

Reading: Matthew 2:1–12

Our reading recounts the compelling narrative of the magi's pilgrimage. Having seen the star, these eastern sojourners journeyed far in search of the newborn king. Their quest draws our attention to the profound truths embedded in this chapter.

The magi, typically regarded as wise men or scholars, weren't Jews, yet they were among the first to seek and worship Jesus. This chapter illustrates God's expansive embrace, hinting at the gospel's inclusivity. The salvation promised isn't just for a select group but for all. This inclusivity foreshadows Jesus's future ministry to outsiders and the marginalized.

Like the magi, the Spirit calls us to undertake a journey. Their adventure wasn't just geographical; it was spiritual. Drawn by a celestial signal, they remind us that God communicates, beckoning us closer. Sometimes, the signs are evident, like a brilliant star, but often, they're subtle nudges within our spirit. The journey might demand sacrifices, but the destination, finding Jesus, promises fulfillment.

The magi's encounter with Herod is a stern reminder of the world's contrasting responses to God's redemptive plan. Herod's trepidation and subsequent malevolence towards the Christ child underscore the age-old conflict between the world's powers and God's kingdom. As disciples of Christ, we follow the Messiah who champions peace, justice, and reconciliation, often juxtaposed against the diseased and dysfunctional imaginations and actions of the world's transient rulers and dominions.

The gifts of the magi—gold, frankincense, and myrrh— weren't mere tokens of wealth. They epitomized Christ's kingship, priestly role, and eventual suffering. Thus, our offerings to the world should echo these themes—alerting everyone everywhere to the rule and reign of God in Christ, interceding in prayer for a broken humanity, and embracing cruciform discipleship. Gold symbolizes our call to serve with integrity and humility, ac- knowledging Christ's reign. Often used in worship, frankincense prompts us to infuse our daily activities with prayer, constantly aspiring for a deeper communion with God. Myrrh, a burial spice, is a stark reminder of Christ's sacrifice and our mandate to exhibit unwavering love and compassion, even in adversity.

Big Idea: Seek earnestly for Christ in every aspect of life, letting his transformative power shape your path and offerings to the world.

Reflection: Like the magi, are there stars—divine signals—guiding you today that you might've overlooked? How can you offer your gifts of "gold," "frankincense," and "myrrh" to better serve your community and reflect Christ's love?

Prayer: Creator God, as the star led the magi to Jesus, illuminate our paths, drawing us closer to you. As we journey through life, help us discern your divine signals and grant us the courage to follow them. May our offerings mirror your love, mercy, and compassion, impacting our world for your kingdom. In Jesus's name, amen.

Day 4

Showing Compassion Amid the Shadows of Empires

Reading: Matthew 2:13-15

In Matthew 2:13-15, we are thrust into a profound moment: an unsettling scene where Joseph, led by a divine dream, takes his young family to Egypt to escape the murderous intent of King Herod. This story echoes Israel's exile to Egypt and foreshadows Christ's redemptive work.

This episode alerts us to an underlying theme in Scripture—God with us, even in flight, even in fear, even amid persecution and violence, even in foreign lands, and even in chaotic, messy, anxiety-producing, disorienting experiences. God is steadfastly present with us. Even amid the oppressive shadows of empires and during times of physical or spiritual exile, God remains unwaveringly with us, guiding and comforting.

This narrative beckons us to consider the nature of our journey with Christ. Are we prepared for the wilderness and spiritual exile? Jesus, even as an infant, wasn't insulated from the world's dangers but, instead, was an embodiment of hope and God's redemption within them. It's a clarion call to deep-rooted faith undeterred by external challenges.

Jesus's brief status as "an internally displaced person" amplifies a consistent biblical theme: caring for the marginalized and advocating for those treated unjustly by worldly powers and empires. This isn't just a historical story; it's a present-day invitation. More than one hundred million people are forcibly displaced—refugees, asylum-seekers, and undocumented migrants. Almost four hundred thousand children are born as refugees each year. They are our brothers and sisters, journeying, like Jesus once did, seeking welcome, safety, protection, and sustenance. When we welcome them, we're welcoming Jesus.

If we genuinely desire to share our faith in Jesus, it is not enough to merely speak of God's love. We must embody it, especially towards those whom society often overlooks. This means a readiness to stand in solidarity with the suffering and to embrace radical compassion.

But we can't do any of this in our strength. We need the grace and presence of Jesus to help us show compassion amid cold, oppressive, dehumanizing empires and systems.

Big Idea: Amid the shadows of empires, may we embody Jesus's radical compassion in every act and encounter.

Reflection: In what ways has your faith journey felt like an unexpected exile, and how have you seen God's presence in those moments? How can you actively embody the love and humility of Christ in engaging with the marginalized in your community?

Prayer: Gracious God, like the young Messiah fleeing to Egypt, many today seek refuge and hope. Open our hearts to see you in their stories. Embolden us to journey into the unfamiliar, leaning on your grace, reflecting your love. May our lives bear witness to the Christ who walked in humility and served in love. Amen.

Day 5

Navigating Turmoil with Divine Assurance

Reading: Matthew 2:16-23

Matthew's second chapter juxtaposes terror and hope, darkness and light. Herod, the embodiment of worldly power, stricken with fear and jealousy, orders the slaughter of innocent children, hoping to eradicate the newly-born King of the Jews.

What strikes us first is the overwhelming violence—a world not so different from ours. The vulnerability of Jesus's family is juxtaposed with Herod's ironfisted and violent rule. Yet, it speaks deeply into our spiritual lives. We, too, feel vulnerable at times, caught in the crossfire of worldly powers, struggling against forces of pride, jealousy, and self-protection. In Colossians, Paul says Christ in you is the hope of glory. But, like Herod, the powers of this world try to squash the burgeoning Christ within us. However, Jesus's survival in this passage affirms this marvelous truth: the light of Christ within us cannot be extinguished.

We often encounter various "Herods" that try to suppress love, humility, and compassion. The path of discipleship is not devoid of Herodian forces. These forces oppose, persecute, and express hostility toward Christ's disciples, seeking to disrupt, destroy, and cause despair. Yet, amid the darkness, we find assurance in

God's providential care, comforting presence, and steadfast love. Even as we traverse the rocky terrains of life—in a world often marred by violence, injustice, and hostility—God's loving, protective hand remains upon us, guiding us toward his grace, love, and fulfilled promises.

We can hope and trust that God will conform us to Christ's image so that "it is no longer I that live, but Christ lives in me" (Gal 2:20). Even in the face of worldly opposition and violence, the divine story of Jesus Christ unfolds uninterrupted. The resilient love of Christ, who was once a vulnerable child, now enables us, empowering us with grace to be faithful disciples amid life's challenges. His love reassures us, reminding us that even in the bleakest moments, God is at work, weaving redemption and renewal. So, we can rest in God's grace as we face worldly powers and life's challenges.

Big Idea: Worldly forces often oppose Christ's followers, but God gives us divine assurance of his presence, providence, and protection, enabling us to rest in God's grace and care.

Reflection: What can you do daily to cultivate spiritual resilience to stand against the "Herods" in your life? As you reflect on the journey of Jesus's family, in what tangible ways are you inspired to engage the world with compassion and truth despite the forces that resist?

Prayer: Lord Jesus, our refuge and strength, remind us that even in the shadows of worldly powers, your light continues to shine. Guide us as we navigate the tumults of life, ensuring that our actions and words always reflect your love, humility, and compassion. Your love and grace empower and guide us. Amen.

Day 6

Embracing Repentance, Renewal, and the Spirit's Fire

Reading: Matthew 3:1–12

In the rugged wilderness landscape of Matthew 3:1–12, John the Baptist emerges, proclaiming a baptism of repentance for the forgiveness of sins. This chapter is rich with symbolic imagery and prophecy fulfillment. John's presence embodies the voice crying out in the wilderness, preparing the way for the Lord. The biblical meaning lies in the unfolding of God's plan, revealing the profound need for inner transformation and readiness for the coming Messiah.

Repentance and humility lay the foundation for this spiritual preparedness, leading us to embrace the grace and love of Christ. The call to repentance invites us to a profound inner transformation, turning our hearts, minds, and actions away from sin and towards God's holiness, love, and transformed life. Repentance is a journey of humility, acknowledging human frailty, and earnestly seeking forgiveness and renewal. This transformation depends entirely on God's grace and the sanctifying and regenerating work of the Spirit of Christ. Repentance is a commitment to align your heart, mind, priorities, and actions with the compassionate, righteous, and just ways of Jesus Christ our Lord. Baptism symbolizes the cleansing of our hearts, making us pure and ready to receive Jesus.

At the core, this chapter centers on the impending ministry of Jesus, who surpasses John and his baptism in every way. Jesus baptizes with the Holy Spirit and fire—empowering and transforming our lives, refining and purifying us from sin and impurity, making us more like Jesus, and filling us with passion and zeal for service, witness, and worship. The winnowing fork and threshing floor image reminds us that the loving Christ is also the holy Lord who separates the righteous from the unrighteous at the final judgment.

The narrative of Matthew 3 points us toward Jesus, reaffirming his love, empowerment, and grace. John the Baptist says that Jesus will baptize us with his Holy Spirit and empowering, purifying fire. Jesus enables us to be his disciples, aligning our lives with his divine will and enabling us to show the world God's extravagant love and transformative gospel truth. Jesus offers us his grace, righteousness, and power, which enable us to repent, believe, and have cleansed hearts. Jesus the Messiah empowers us for righteous, repentant, loving, humble, just, Spirit-empowered discipleship that glorifies God.

Big Idea: Embrace humility and repentance, allowing the transformative love and grace of Jesus to cleanse, renew, and empower your daily walk in love, justice, and service.

Reflection: How do the themes of repentance and baptism echo in your heart today? How can you open yourself up more fully to God's empowering presence?

Prayer: Dear Jesus, grant us the humility to embrace repentance. Please cleanse our spirits and reignite our hearts and paths with the brilliance of your power, love, and grace. Amen.

Day 7

The Waters of Obedience and Love

Reading: Matthew 3:13-17

In Matthew 3:13-17, we stand on the banks of the Jordan River, witnessing the baptism of Jesus. This chapter marks the beginning of his public ministry. It calls our attention to the unveiling of God's Son, obediently stepping into the waters of baptism. It's an invitation to contemplate the profound humility and the immense love Jesus embodies.

The heavens part, and God's voice affirms Jesus, setting him apart and designating him as the chosen one. It speaks of divine love, approval, identity, and mission. Descending like a dove, the Holy Spirit represents peace, promise, and the beginning of a new creation. It harks back to the Old Testament images of the Spirit hovering over the waters, bringing life and order out of chaos.

The Father's words reveal the profound, boundless love within the Trinity—between Father, Son, and Holy Spirit—a steadfast, self-giving, and eternal love. This moment extends an invitation to each one of us. As the Father loves the Son, so are we lavishly loved. In the act of Jesus's baptism, we glimpse the unity and love within the Trinity, a love that overflows and extends to humanity, to you and me. We are invited into this divine dance of mutual love, honor, and joy.

The baptism of Jesus beckons us to enter a rhythm of death and resurrection, a pattern of letting go and receiving anew. It encourages believers to embrace a journey of continual transformation, undergirded by the sustaining grace of Christ. As we submerge ourselves in the living waters of faith, we are enveloped by Jesus's love, equipped to emerge as ambassadors of peace and reconciliation.

Just as Jesus submitted to baptism, we, too, are invited to bow low, recognize our shared humanity, and work ardently for the well-being of all. Our interactions ought to mirror the self-giving love of Jesus, extending grace and fostering connections that heal and unite.

Big Idea: Step boldly into the boundless love of the Father, Son, and Spirit, allowing this love to transform you into a beacon of divine love, unity, and grace.

Reflection: Are we allowing the grace and love of Jesus to permeate and transform our lives? How are we embodying humility and divine love in our relationships?

Prayer: Gracious God, as we meditate on the baptism of Jesus, stir within us a renewed commitment to follow his example. Infuse us with his love, grace, and humility. Rooted in your love, may our lives echo your redemptive work, mirroring the life of Jesus. Embolden us to share your peace, justice, and love in a fragmented world. As the Spirit descended upon Jesus, may your Spirit enliven our souls. Amen.

Day 8

Embracing the Wilderness

Reading: Matthew 4:1-11

In this story, we journey alongside Jesus into the barren wilderness, a place of vulnerability and solitude. This stark backdrop, painted with hues of challenge and temptation, reveals how profoundly the natural, human, and spiritual realities are intertwined. The tempter surfaces, engaging Jesus in a battle of identity and mission, presenting allurements of power, prestige, and security. Yet, in every encounter, Jesus resolutely anchors himself in the Scriptures and his relationship with God, unveiling the profound mystery that true identity and power are found in humility, service, and utter dependence on God.

This passage summons us into a transformative solitude where we face our vulnerabilities and temptations. It is here, in the silence of the wilderness, that our true identity is both challenged and affirmed. The world's promises of authority, admiration, and assurance beckon us, their allure often clouding our vision and distorting our path. Yet, echoing through the canyons of our soul is the gentle whisper of Jesus, calling us back to the simplicity of faith, a reliance not on the tangible but on the Eternal One.

Solitude, silence, and contemplation often move us toward action. Rooted in prayer and self-examination, this action and service is characterized by humility, dependence on God, and an unwavering commitment to righteousness, justice, compassion, and love. This path is not passive; it is an active, deliberate choice to serve others, offer forgiveness generously, and promote justice. Jesus's encounter in the wilderness gives us the resolve to confront the tempter's allurements with unwavering faith in God and the power of Scripture. Jesus's example in the wilderness gives us the courage to respond to the world's afflictions with the healing balm of love, compassion, and humble service. We are reminded that the kingdom of God breaks through not in displays of worldly power but in acts of selfless love and mercy.

In Jesus's love, we find the strength to traverse our wilderness. His enabling grace equips us to face our vulnerabilities, discern the hollow allure of worldly temptation, and choose the path of humble service and love. The story of Jesus's temptation beckons us to a transformed life, anchored in his love and lived out in his grace for his glory.

Big Idea: Embrace the wilderness of life, anchoring your soul in God's word, to resist temptation and walk the humble path of love and service.

Reflection: How does the wilderness experience speak to your vulnerabilities and temptations? Where is Jesus inviting you to relinquish worldly allurements and embrace a path of humility and service?

Prayer: Gracious God, lead us through the wilderness of our journey. Strengthen us in the face of temptation, and root us deeply in your boundless love and grace. May we walk humbly, serve selflessly, and love unconditionally as reflections of Jesus, our guide and savior. Amen.

Day 9

Jesus Reveals Good News Holistically

Reading: Matthew 4:12–25

This story tells of the commencement of Jesus's ministry, calling his first disciples, and performing healings. The light has dawned, bringing hope and restoration. The sun rises on humanity in the glorious person of Jesus and the brilliant hope and shalom of his kingdom.

We see Jesus proclaiming the gospel, the good news that God's kingdom has broken into our world, calling us to repentance and a transformed life. Our role as disciples is crystallized. The call of the first disciples mirrors our summons to lay aside the nets of our desires, securities, and fears, embracing the profound adventure of following Jesus. Our spiritual lives bloom in this earnest following, a journey of constant learning, loving, and living in his divine light.

In this story, the holistic nature of Jesus's mission and ministry unveils itself as a seamless tapestry woven with teaching, proclaiming, and healing threads. Jesus traversed the regions, entering synagogues and communities (religious and societal spaces) with the transformative message of the kingdom's nearness.

But his gospel did not halt at words; his gospel manifested as tangible, compassionate actions and healings. This holistic approach shows the expansive breath of Jesus's ministry, melding spiritual proclamation with physical restoration. His mission, steeped in love and compassion, crossed boundaries, offering wholeness to the wounded, fractured, and marginalized.

Jesus proclaimed the good news of the kingdom holistically, showing that the gospel message is not confined to spiritual salvation alone but extends to the transformation and healing of communities, societies, and creation. Jesus recognized the multifaceted nature of human existence, addressing spiritual, social, emotional, physical, and economic needs. He shows us that our ministry and mission must be about the unfolding (the revealing) of the whole gospel to the whole person and the whole world. We point people to Jesus, the light who has dawned, and his kingdom that is near.

As followers of Jesus, this holistic essence should shape our ministry and mission. We must emulate Jesus's integral (holistic) approach, intertwining word and deed, ensuring our proclamation of good news is complemented by loving, just, reconciling, and healing actions. In this way, our ministry blossoms, reflecting the multifaceted, holistic heart of Jesus's mission, extending his light of restoration and hope into every corner of our world.

Big Idea: Imitate Jesus through a holistic approach to declaring his gospel and kingdom. Matthew 4 shows us that this holistic way of service includes: (1) proclaiming the good news of the kingdom, (2) teaching about Jesus Christ and his gospel, (3) performing miraculous signs as God enables, and (4) engaging in healing and compassionate actions.

Reflection: What nets do you need to lay aside (desires, securities, and fears) so that you can follow Jesus? How can you complement your proclamation of good news with loving, just, reconciling, and healing actions?

Prayer: Creator God, please grant us the courage and wisdom to embody Jesus's holistic approach in our lives, ensuring that our proclamation of your good news is complemented by loving, just, reconciling, and healing actions. Amen.

Day 10

Living the Beatitudes

Reading: Matthew 5:1–12

Matthew 5:1–12, the opening of the Sermon on the Mount, paints a beautiful and paradoxical picture of the blessed life. Known as the Beatitudes, Jesus proclaims blessings on the poor in spirit, those who mourn, the meek, those who hunger and thirst for righteousness, the merciful, the pure in heart, the peacemakers, and those who are persecuted for righteousness' sake. This passage beckons us to a profound, upside-down kingdom where the last are first and the first are last.

Jesus, in his boundless love and grace, is not merely offering guidance on the spiritual life but is honoring those in his upside-down kingdom. He declares that the kingdom of God is vibrantly alive among the humble, the merciful, and the peacemakers, affirming their invaluable role and presence in the unfolding realm of divine love and justice.

In these verses, the biblical meaning emerges as a manifesto of the kingdom of heaven. Jesus is redefining blessedness, turning worldly ideas upside down. The world prizes influence, power, acclaim, wealth, and triumph, but Jesus speaks of humility, mourning, and peace. These heart attitudes draw us into a deeper relationship with God, showing us that our spiritual vitality depends entirely on God's grace.

The Beatitudes teach us not only about our relationship with God but also about discipleship. In the call to be peacemakers and the blessedness of the persecuted, we find a commitment to justice, reconciliation, and love for neighbors and enemies alike. The pursuit of righteousness leads to peace, not just for us but for our communities and the world. By embodying the Beatitudes, we demonstrate an alternative way of life that confronts the world's brokenness with the gospel's healing and hope.

These Beatitudes guide us spiritually, reminding us that the Christian journey is not about achieving power or success but embodying humility, righteousness, and mercy. In being poor in spirit, meek, and merciful, we reflect the character of Jesus, revealing his transformative love and grace to a world in desperate need. We are empowered to live this out not through our strength but through the enabling grace of Jesus Christ, who perfectly embodied the Beatitudes in his life, death, and resurrection.

Big Idea: Embrace humility, seek righteousness, and embody peace as active bearers of Christ's transformative love and grace.

Reflection: How is God calling you to embody the Beatitudes in your life and community? In what ways are you being invited to depend more fully on the grace of Jesus Christ?

Prayer: Gracious God, as we meditate on the Beatitudes, we recognize our utter dependence on your grace. Strengthen us to walk in the way of Jesus, embracing humility, righteousness, and peace. May our lives bear witness to the transformative power of your love and grace in the world. In Jesus's name, amen.

Day 11

Being Salt and Light

Reading: Matthew 5:13-16

In ancient times, salt was valued for preserving qualities, a defense against decay. Light dispels darkness, unveiling truth and direction. The call to be salt and light is a summons to a life of Christlike influence, actively combating moral decay and bringing clarity and hope to a world shrouded in darkness. But this isn't about grasping after acclaim, power, control, or worldly influence. Transforming lives and society emerges from the wellspring of humble service and love. It's in the small, selfless acts of care and compassion that true change is most often birthed, radiating God's love and gently shaping the world anew.

The metaphor of salt and light reflects our purpose and mission as followers of Christ. We are entrusted with reflecting Christ's light in the world, permeating our surroundings with his love, truth, and grace, and actively preserving the goodness and justice he embodies. We are called into dynamic participation in God's redemptive work as conduits of his love and grace.

Salt is also about flavor—followers of Jesus enhance the delightful, joyous flavors of grace, shalom, and goodness in the world, offering a foretaste of the flavors of the kingdom of heaven.

The call to be salt and light is not passive. It propels us into the world as change agents, promoting peace, justice, and love. In every interaction, we're invited to mirror the humble, servant-hearted love of Jesus, to be advocates for justice and reconciliation, reflecting the gospel's transformative power. This identity informs and shapes our relationship with the world, guiding us in embodying the love, humility, and grace of Jesus in every situation.

In Matthew 5:13–16, Jesus calls his followers to inhabit a life in harmony with the gospel, a life that holds a preserving influence morally, socially, and culturally in our society. We may face opposition and persecution, and many will reject the gospel. Despite this, the beauty of Christian living will shine, drawing others into the light and leading them to praise God. Following Jesus is not about seizing power or control but embodying a life of loving, selfless service.

In fulfilling this divine call, we're not abandoned to our devices. Jesus, the true light of the world, infuses us with his strength, enabling us to shine his light and be salt in the world. His grace and love empower and sustain us, ensuring that our light does not dim, and our salt does not lose its savor.

Big Idea: Embrace your identity as salt and light, actively infusing every corner of the world with the preserving and illuminating love of Jesus.

Reflection: How is the call to be salt and light shaping your engagement with the world? How are you bringing preservation and illumination into your sphere of influence?

Prayer: Dear Lord, embolden us to embrace our identity as the salt and light in this world. Infuse us with your strength and grace so that we may reflect your love, peace, and justice in all we do. Let our lives continually point to you, the source of all light and life. Amen.

Day 12

Delving Deeper into the Heart

Reading: Matthew 5:17-37

Our journey through the Gospel of Matthew takes us to a challenging stretch of Scripture. Christ proclaims, "Don't think that I came to destroy the law or the prophets. I didn't come to destroy, but to fulfill" (v. 17). But as we read through the Sermon on the Mount, we discern an intensification of the law, pressing more profoundly into the heart's terrain.

First, the biblical meanings of the chapter are striking. Here, Jesus isn't merely updating the Mosaic law. Instead, he calls us beyond external compliance to an inner transformation. No longer is it sufficient to avoid the act of murder; harboring anger places one in jeopardy. Physical adultery isn't the sole transgression; the lustful gaze condemns just as severely. Jesus probes the motivations and desires that drive our actions, highlighting that genuine righteousness is a matter of the heart.

Such a revelation dramatically shifts the landscape of our spiritual lives. Many of us, if candid, might acknowledge the ease with which we follow external regulations. But when the lens shifts inward, the shadows of our hearts become glaringly evident. No longer can we hide behind a facade of outward obedience. Instead, the call is to radical inner transformation, where every thought and intent aligns with God's heart.

The Sermon on the Mount invites us to live in the righteousness of God's kingdom—a radical new way of life shaped around Jesus's teachings and example. Jesus says the kingdom of God is a spiritual kingdom of exemplary humility, nonviolence, righteousness, justice, truthfulness, and compassion—virtues only possible through faith in Jesus Christ and dependence on his Spirit. Repentance and humility, integrity and truth-telling, righteousness and compassion, love for enemies and nonviolence, rejecting materialism and worldly values—these challenge the world's values, and we can only achieve this countercultural, radical new way of life in the power of Jesus Christ.

In relationships, the challenge is to love, forgive, and serve with the same depth and intensity Christ loves us. This is not mere human effort. It's an outpouring of grace, an overflow of the heart transformed by Christ. After all, Jesus empowers us to live out the righteousness and radical way of life taught in the Sermon on the Mount.

This passage moves our gaze to the crucified and risen Lord. His love and grace are our foundation. He understands our struggles and beckons us to rely on him, for by his enabling alone, we can genuinely love our neighbors and enemies, serve others selflessly, and exhibit a heart-transformed righteousness.

Big Idea: Embrace inner transformation, aligning every motive with Christ's teachings, to authentically live a kingdom-driven, countercultural life empowered by his grace.

Reflection: In what areas have you been content with external obedience, neglecting the call to heart transformation? How might a deeper embrace of Jesus's love and grace empower you to live authentically and with love?

Prayer: Lord Jesus, as we delve into the depths of your call, may we not be overwhelmed but find our refuge in your grace. Teach us to love and serve with the intensity and purity you embody. Grant us hearts aligned

with yours, that our every action may resonate with your heart's beat.
Amen.

Day 13

A Revolutionary Love

Reading: Matthew 5:38-48

In this passage, Jesus turns established norms on their head. In our polarized age, where people throw insults at each other online, and enemies seem to lurk around every ideological corner, Jesus challenges us to be different. A cross-shaped (cruciform) love is astonishing, extravagant, and countercultural. If you say you love God, don't just offer love to fellow believers, neighbors, and strangers; go much further—"But I tell you, love your enemies, bless those who curse you, do good to those who hate you, and pray for those who spitefully use you and persecute you, that you may be sons of your Father who is in heaven" (v. 44-45).

The profound biblical meanings of this chapter are both unsettling and transformative. Where the world seeks retribution, Jesus proposes a non-retaliatory love. Instead of reciprocating violence with violence, Christ beckons us to offer the other cheek and to go the extra mile. It's a love that dares to embrace even our enemies, a love so radical that it seems almost impractical.

Jesus offers us a transformative love and invites us to imitate that love in revolutionary and countercultural ways. For our spiritual lives, this is a clarion call to a more profound, cruciform, sacrificial love that transcends human reasoning and ability. It's not about suppressing our feelings of hurt or bypassing justice. Instead, it's an invitation to see as Christ sees, to recognize the *imago Dei*, the image of God, even in those who oppose us. Such a perspective is no mere ethical code; it's a heart transformation rooted in divine love.

But how do we let this shape our engagement with the world? In a polarized and conflicted culture that often shouts, "us vs. them," Jesus reminds us of the way of the cross and the kingdom of God. It's about dismantling barriers, restoring relationships, and fostering a community where love overrides divisions. This love isn't passive; it actively seeks peace, justice, and reconciliation. Such love for enemies imitates the gracious and self-giving love of Jesus—a love that does not merely respond in kind but actively seeks the well-being of the other, even when it's undeserved. Doing so becomes a potent testament to the gospel's transformative power.

At the center of this revolutionary love stands Jesus. His life, death, and resurrection epitomize this self-giving love. He didn't retaliate against his accusers but bore our sins on the cross, offering forgiveness and grace. It's in the shadow of the cross and the glow of the empty tomb that we find the strength and enabling to live out this radical love.

Big Idea: Live out Christ's revolutionary love, transcending retaliation to seek peace and reconciliation even with those who oppose us.

Reflection: Where have you struggled to show love to those who oppose or hurt you? How can deeply contemplating Christ's love for you radically empower you to love others?

Prayer: Lord Jesus, you have loved us with a love beyond comprehension. Teach our hearts to love as you have loved. May our lives reflect your revolutionary love, tearing down walls and building bridges, all for the sake of your kingdom. In your empowering name, we pray. Amen.

Day 14

True Righteousness from the Heart

Reading: Matthew 6:1–18

Journeying through Matthew's Gospel, we find ourselves confronted by Jesus's profound teachings on the nature of true righteousness. In Matthew 6:1–18, Jesus doesn't merely call for religious acts; he reaches into the depths of our hearts, challenging the very motives that drive us.

Jesus warns against practicing righteousness to garner human approval. He presents a paradigm shift—our spiritual acts, whether giving, praying, or fasting, are not for public applause but for an audience of one. Jesus reveals that what really matters is the condition of our hearts.

This passage reminds us that God values authenticity. It's tempting to wear masks, to cultivate an external image while neglecting inner transformation. Yet, in the secret place, away from the world's gaze, we find genuine communion with God. Acts like prayer and fasting are not mere rituals but opportunities for intimate engagement with our Creator.

The Lord's Prayer encapsulates genuine faith, emphasizes heart motives over mere acts, warns against hypocrisy, promotes intimate communion with God, champions forgiveness, positions worship and prayer as heart-centered devotion, and underscores our profound dependence on God's grace. Jesus's prayer invites us to live in ways that glorify God and serve God's will and kingdom.

As we consider how this passage informs our interaction with the world, we see that genuine, heart-driven righteousness creates ripple effects. A heart in tune with God naturally extends forgiveness as it understands the depth of forgiveness it has received. Such a heart strives for peace and reconciliation, not out of duty but from an overflow of God's love. Our interactions, driven by true righteousness, become marked by humility, compassion, and genuine service to others.

Central to our ability to live out this heart-transforming righteousness is Jesus himself. By his grace and enabling, we can move beyond mere external acts to cultivate a genuine relationship with God. In Jesus, we find the perfect embodiment of humility and selfless love, offering us both the example and the empowerment to walk this path.

Big Idea: Cultivate authentic heart-driven righteousness, seeking God's approval in secret spaces, and let it transform your daily interactions with the world.

Reflection: When have you found yourself performing spiritual acts for the sake of appearances? How might a deeper focus on heart transformation reshape your daily interactions?

Prayer: Creator God, thank you for the gift of your Son, Jesus, who shows us the way to true righteousness. Forgive us for the times we've sought human approval over your delight. Mold our hearts so we may reflect your heart to the world in every act, thought, and intention. We pray in the name of Jesus, who empowers and guides us. Amen.

Day 15

Treasures in Heaven and Rest for the Anxious Heart

Reading: Matthew 6:19–34

Matthew 6:19–34 draws our eyes to the reality that our lives are not determined by the material things we gather but by where we place our heart's treasures. In a culture bustling with consumerism and a restless pursuit for the next big thing, Jesus challenges us: "Don't lay up treasures for yourselves on the earth . . . but lay up for yourselves treasures in heaven" (v. 19–20). This isn't simply about material possessions; it's about our heart's allegiances and desires.

A recurring theme emerges throughout this passage: our treasures reveal our true worship. Where we invest our time, energy, and resources often mirrors where our heart truly lies. Jesus pushes us further, reminding us that no one can serve two masters. You either embrace the world's temporal treasures or cling to God's eternal riches. This is a matter of our heart's loyalty, a spiritual tug-of-war between our human desires and God's divine call.

As we journey with Christ, our spiritual lives find depth when we relinquish our anxieties and trust in God's provision. The birds of the air and the lilies of the field testify to a Creator who provides. They don't worry. They rest in his care. How much more will he care for us, his beloved children? We're invited into a life of deep trust, where our worries are replaced by faith in God's unending provision.

Christ's words inspire a distinctive lifestyle, moving us beyond mere belief to profound embodiment. We're called to a life of peace, knowing God will provide; of justice, by not hoarding resources; of reconciliation, as we free our hearts from materialism to truly love others; and of gospel communication, sharing the good news that true riches lie in God's kingdom. By living in this manner, we not only witness to Jesus but also embrace a love that extends to neighbors and even enemies. We engage in humble service, reflecting the compassion, forgiveness, and grace Jesus has shown us.

Amid our anxieties and desires, Jesus is our ultimate treasure, embodying love, grace, and all we truly need. Through his sacrifice and enabling power, we find the strength to be faithful disciples, responding to God's call over the world's temptations. By abiding in Jesus, we're empowered to live out the themes of this passage, with our eyes fixed on heavenly treasures and our hearts filled with divine love.

Big Idea: Anchor your heart in heavenly treasures, trusting God's provision over worldly anxieties.

Reflection: Where are you storing your treasures? How does your daily life reflect your trust in God's provision?

Prayer: Our Comforter and Provider, please help us to focus on heavenly treasures, to rest in your provision, and to seek your kingdom above all. Let our lives reflect true discipleship, mirroring Jesus's love, grace, and humility. In Christ's name, amen.

Day 16

Grace-Filled Living

Reading: Matthew 7:1–12

Matthew 7:1–12 invites us into an introspective journey. The passage speaks of not judging, seeking God's good gifts, and treating others as we want to be treated—the Golden Rule. But at its core, it's more than just moral directives; it's a call to radical inner transformation.

Judgment begins in the heart. We're inclined to see the speck in others' eyes while overlooking the log in our own. Isn't it easy to see others' faults and remain blind to our own? This isn't a superficial suggestion to simply be "nice." It's about heart postures and the dangers of self-righteousness. The gospel isn't about becoming better judges but recognizing our need for grace.

Why? Because it is by grace that we're healed, loved, honored, and saved. The way we view others reflects our understanding of God's mercy toward us. If we've genuinely encountered God's grace, it should give us an overwhelming desire to show grace to others and pursue reconciliation, peace, and justice. A transformed heart that's encountered Jesus's love can't help but love in return. It's about a reconciled life woven deeply with threads of compassion, forgiveness, and humility.

The passage continues with the idea of asking, seeking, and knocking. God desires good for us—more than we often realize. But God's definition of good isn't rooted in transient pleasures or fleeting successes. It's rooted in God's kingdom—a place where justice prevails, peace reigns, and love is the air we breathe. To live as Christ's disciples means actively seeking his kingdom and righteousness.

However, seeking is more than just asking; it's about aligning our will with God's. The essence of the Christian life is not about attaining but surrendering. As we learn to surrender, we reflect the very heart of Jesus, who loved and embraced neighbors and enemies. Jesus served not out of duty but out of profound love, and so should we.

This profound love leads us to the Golden Rule. At first glance, it seems simple enough—treat others how you'd like to be treated. But its roots go deeper. It's about understanding that every soul we encounter is a bearer of God's image, deserving of respect, love, and dignity. When we see others through this lens, our actions naturally flow from a place of love, inclusion, honor, and service.

But how do we live this out? It's not by sheer willpower or a checklist of good deeds. It's by anchoring our lives in Jesus, allowing his love, enabling, and grace to permeate every facet of our being.

Big Idea: Let God's grace transform your heart, leading you to love and serve others with genuine humility and compassion.

Reflection: In what areas of your life are you quick to judge? How might recognizing God's grace toward you change your perspective? How can you actively seek God's kingdom and righteousness daily?

Prayer: Lord Jesus, you've called us to a higher way of living—one marked by love, grace, and humility. Transform our hearts so that we might reflect your heart to a world in need. Let our lives testify to your grace, and may we be channels of your peace. In your name, we pray, amen.

Day 17

Foundations in Faith

Reading: Matthew 7:13–29

Matthew 7:13–29 presents us with a vivid contrast: wide and narrow gates, true and false prophets, wise and foolish builders. But the profound message woven through these parables is about the substance of genuine faith and the life it births.

Jesus speaks of two gates. The wide gate, though popular, leads to destruction. The narrow gate, while challenging and less chosen, leads to life. This isn't merely about an afterlife but a transformed, abundant life here and now. It's a life anchored in authenticity, humility, the gospel of Jesus Christ, and a robust love for God and neighbor.

But how do we discern the true path? Jesus warns of false prophets. These are not just external threats but internal ones—our desires and inclinations that can steer us away from the heart of the gospel. True spirituality isn't marked by eloquence or show but by the fruit it produces—fruits of peace, justice, compassion, faithfulness to the gospel of Christ, and a relentless pursuit of God's kingdom.

This pursuit requires wisdom. The parable of the builders drives this home. Those who hear and act upon Jesus's words are likened to the wise builder. They lay a foundation that can withstand the torrents of life. It's an active faith deeply embedded in Jesus's teachings, leading us to serve, forgive, and witness with unwavering conviction.

In essence, this passage is an invitation. An invitation to a deeper relationship with Jesus, whose love and grace empower us to walk the narrow path, discern the genuine from the false, and build on a solid foundation.

It is beautifully comforting to know that we aren't navigating this journey through sheer willpower. Instead, we are upheld by Jesus's enabling grace. When we falter, his love restores. When we stray, his mercy guides us. In his strength, we can truly live as peacemakers, champions of justice, and bearers of the gospel message.

Big Idea: Anchor your life in Jesus's teachings, choosing the narrow path of genuine faith that produces fruits of love, justice, and service.

Reflection: In what areas of your life might you choose the wider, easier path? How can you realign with the narrow way Jesus calls us to? What does building on a solid foundation look like in your daily life?

Prayer: Gracious Lord, you call us to a life of genuine faith, marked by love, justice, and service. Strengthen our resolve to choose the narrow path, discern truth from falsehood, and build our lives on the foundation of your word. May we find comfort and guidance in every challenge in your unwavering love. Amen.

Day 18

An Invitation to Healing and Wholeness

Reading: Matthew 8

As we meditate on Matthew 8, we see Jesus's authority manifested, not in majestic displays but through intimate encounters: dignifying and healing the leper, the centurion's servant, Peter's mother-in-law, and others afflicted.

First, the leper's healing is profound. Leprosy in biblical times wasn't just a physical ailment; it was an identity. The afflicted were outcasts. When Jesus touches the leper, he isn't merely healing a skin condition. He is restoring dignity, community, and identity. How often do we, too, carry the "leprosy" of shame, rejection, or brokenness? Jesus reaches out, longing to touch and restore us.

The centurion's faith becomes the focal point in the subsequent narrative. Amid an occupying force, this centurion recognized Jesus's unparalleled authority. He understood his unworthiness yet believed in the Messiah's compassion. In our sense of inadequacy, how might we lean into such unwavering faith, trusting that Jesus can and will intervene?

We're reminded of life's turbulent nature in the calming of the storm. Waves of doubt, anxiety, and fear often threaten to drown us. Yet, amid these storms, Jesus invites us to faith. When we cry,

"Save us, Lord!" he calms our fears, showing that, even in chaos, peace is available to those anchored in him.

This chapter confronts us with demons, showing us the cosmic battle waged around us. Jesus's authority over these dark forces is paramount. But remember, it's not just about overpowering evil; it's about liberation, setting captives free. Our world is rife with oppressive powers—systemic injustices, societal divides, and personal battles. As Christ's ambassadors, we're called to stand against such forces, yearning for justice, reconciliation, peace, and freedom.

This chapter calls us to a discipleship of humility, service, faith, and love. It beckons us to testify to a Jesus who doesn't shun the marginalized but seeks them, a Lord who doesn't rely on powerful oratory but on personal encounters, and a Savior who provides physical relief and profound, holistic transformation.

The Spirit invites us to respond to Jesus's love, enabling, and grace. Will we allow him to touch our deepest wounds, calm our fiercest storms, and expel our darkest demons?

Big Idea: Actively seek Jesus's transformative touch in every storm, knowing he brings healing and wholeness.

Reflection: Where in your life are you longing for Jesus's touch, healing, and restoration? What "storms" are you currently navigating? How can you anchor yourself in Christ's peace amid the chaos?

Prayer: Lord Jesus, thank you for revealing your authority, not in grandeur but grace. May we recognize our need for your touch, lean into your peace, and stand with you in seeking justice and reconciliation. Empower us to lead lives anchored in faith, humility, and love. Amen.

Day 19

Paralysis, Pardon, and the People's Physician

Reading: Matthew 9:1–13

In Matthew 9:1–13, we glimpse the profound commingling of the physical and spiritual in Christ's ministry. In healing the paralyzed man, Jesus showcases his power over bodily afflictions and notably emphasizes spiritual restoration—forgiving sins.

At the core, this narrative is a poignant unveiling of our deepest malaise—spiritual paralysis. Aren't we, too, like the paralyzed man, at times crippled not just by life's external adversities but by the weight of our sins and failings? As Jesus gazes into the soul of the paralyzed man, our Lord discerns that he needs mobility but, more profoundly, yearns for mending in the fractured places of his spirit. The gasps of the onlookers aren't just at the miracle of restored movement; it's the audacious declaration, "Your sins are forgiven."

How this informs our spiritual walk is manifold. It compels us to look inward, recognizing our own spiritual immobility. It's easy, after all, to get ensnared in the rhythm of religious motions while our hearts remain stagnant, untouched by the vivifying waters of Christ's love. But here lies the challenge and the invitation: to let

Christ's gaze penetrate our veneers, acknowledge our brokenness, and seek his healing touch in the places we often hide.

If the narrative ended there, it would be more than enough. But it doesn't. The subsequent calling of Matthew, a tax collector, jolts us from complacency. Christ's table fellowship with "sinners" wasn't a mere act of rebellion against religious elites. It was a powerful testament to his radical, inclusive love that beckons us to break barriers, dine with the "other," and embody reconciliation.

What, then, does this mean for how we should live? Discipleship isn't a self-fueled endeavor. Jesus will always be the people's physician, healing the broken with love, inclusion, and grace. Moreover, the same Jesus who beckoned Matthew away from his tax booth enables us by his grace to walk in step with his heart. He not only offers the invitation but also the empowerment. Thus, our response to Matthew 9:1–13 isn't merely admiration but imitation, leaning into Jesus's love and letting it mold our every step.

Big Idea: Embrace Jesus Christ's healing touch in personal brokenness and actively extend his inclusive love to all, especially the marginalized.

Reflection: In what areas of your life do you sense spiritual paralysis, and how can you invite Jesus Christ into those spaces for healing and restoration? How are you being called to emulate Jesus's inclusive love, breaking barriers and reaching out to those different from you?

Prayer: Loving Jesus, healer of our souls, help us recognize our own paralysis and lean into your transforming touch. May we marvel at your miracles and act on your redemptive love. Equip us to embody compassion, humility, and service, seeing others through your eyes. In your name, we pray. Amen.

Day 20

A Call to Embrace God's Heartbeat

Reading: Matthew 9:14–38

In Matthew 9:14–38, a story unfolds revealing Jesus's heartbeat—compassion. In every narrative fragment, from fasting to raising the dead, a Jesus emerges who meets people in their depths. He perceives their pain, understands their questions, and offers radical responses.

First, consider the question of fasting. Why aren't Jesus's disciples fasting when John's are? Jesus answers with an invitation to understand times and seasons. When the bridegroom is present, it's a time for joy, not mourning. There's a profound invitation here, beckoning us into the rhythms of God's kingdom. Jesus implies there's a time for everything—a time for mourning, yes, but also a time for joy. We cultivate spiritual vitality by discerning these seasons.

Following this, Jesus demonstrates his authority to forgive sins. Such authority baffles and challenges the status quo. We're shown that the real paralysis isn't always physical. Sometimes, it's the weight of unforgiveness, of guilt and shame. To experience freedom, we need a more profound healing that reconciles us to God and others.

When Jesus sees the harassed and helpless crowds, he is moved with compassion. This isn't mere pity; it's a gut-wrenching, heart-stirring response. Jesus sees people not as projects or numbers but as the beloved, yearning for shepherds.

How, then, should this inform the Christian walk? First, we must embrace a lifestyle of discernment—discerning the seasons of life and responding appropriately. Engaging in spiritual disciplines, like fasting, should arise from a desire to align with God's rhythms, not just religious rituals.

Secondly, recognize that our call to justice and peace begins in the realm of the heart. Before we can be agents of external reconciliation, we must first experience the internal peace of being forgiven and forgiving others.

Lastly, and most significantly, our lives should pulsate with compassion. Such compassion isn't passive; it's active. It sees the pain in the world and moves towards it, driven by a deep love and an unwavering faith in the transformative power of Jesus.

For this is the crux: it is in Jesus that we find the grace and strength to live out these truths. His love enables us to love neighbors and enemies. We can serve Jesus and others with humility and compassion by his grace. As Jesus says, "The harvest indeed is plentiful, but the laborers are few" (v. 37). Jesus enables us to go out with love and the gospel of grace into a field of hearts yearning for healing, kindness, and compassion.

Big Idea: Live attuned to God's rhythms, letting Jesus's compassion drive you towards healing and reconciliation in the world.

Reflection: Do you need to discern God's rhythms better? How can you align more closely with them? Where might God be calling you to demonstrate compassion? How can you move toward pain, bearing the love and hope of Jesus?

Prayer: Lord Jesus, thank you for revealing the deep wells of compassion. Teach us to discern your rhythms, embrace your forgiveness, and walk in the compassionate way you've shown us. May our lives resonate with your heartbeat, drawing others closer to you. Amen.

Day 21

The Sending and the Cost of Discipleship

Reading: Matthew 10

In Matthew 10, Jesus summons his twelve disciples, empowers them, and dispatches them to the lost sheep of Israel. This chapter unfurls like a rich tapestry, detailing the mandate, the mission, and the mayhem they might face.

This passage is a profound reflection on discipleship. It speaks of both empowerment and cost. The disciples are granted authority to cast out unclean spirits and heal, showcasing God's kingdom breaking into our reality. But Jesus also warns of the inevitable challenges they, and by extension, all disciples, will face. These challenges include societal rejection, family division, and personal persecution. And yet, amid these warnings, Christ reassures them of his unwavering presence and provision. "Are not two sparrows sold for a penny? Yet none of them will fall to the ground outside your Father's care."

The chapter reminds us that our spiritual journey isn't about serenity but fidelity and trust amid the storms. The world often opposes the values of the kingdom. Yet, we are to remain steadfast. Jesus states that he did not come to bring peace but a sword. Not that he champions conflict, but that the nature of his mission—where love confronts evil, and light dispels darkness—might lead to discord. There's a sense of juxtaposition, a call to peace and reconciliation on the one hand and an acknowledgment of the inevitable disturbances the gospel would cause on the other.

Matthew 10 depicts a Messiah introducing a countercultural kingdom, radically subverting worldly norms. Through Christ's teachings and commissioning of disciples, he upends societal expectations, asserting that true power lies in humility, service, and self-sacrifice, challenging and disrupting conventional paradigms of power and allegiance.

We might face opposition in our quest for justice, truth, and love. Our lives might bear witness to Christ in ways that disrupt societal norms. But Jesus reminds us of the value of humility, the art of listening, and the power of serving others. The disciple's journey isn't merely about grand gestures but about faithfully living out the gospel in daily, ordinary life—by showing compassion, forgiveness, and love even to our perceived enemies. These acts witness to a kingdom and a Messiah, not of this world.

Big Idea: Live boldly as disciples, drawing strength from Christ's love, as you embody the values of God's kingdom amid adversity.

Reflection: In what areas of your life do you feel the tension of being a disciple? How can you embody the values of the kingdom in your daily interactions?

Prayer: Loving Jesus, you call us into a profound journey of discipleship. Grant us the wisdom to navigate its challenges, the humility to serve, and the courage to remain steadfast. May we be witnesses to your redemptive love and grace in all we do. Amen.

Day 22

Rhythms of Divine Restfulness

Reading: Matthew 11

Matthew 11 presents a vivid scene, a moment in Jesus's ministry laden with questions, surprises, and invitations. John the Baptist, locked behind prison bars, dispatches disciples with a question that resonates with anyone who's ever yearned for the Messiah's arrival: "Are you the one who is to come, or should we expect someone else?" It's not simply a query about identity but one pregnant with the ache of hope deferred and the weight of expectation.

In response, Jesus doesn't provide a direct answer. Instead, he offers a canvas of signs and wonders that are unmistakably messianic. In these acts, the deeper rhythms of God's kingdom emerge. The marginalized, oppressed, and downtrodden are seen and restored, emphasizing the Creator's heart for justice, reconciliation, healing, and compassion.

Yet, the most striking exhortation comes as Jesus beckons: "Come to me, all you who are weary and burdened, and I will give you rest." This isn't a poetic, abstract offer but a tangible lifeline for those drowning under life's pressures. It's a call to find refuge in the loving embrace of the humble teacher from Nazareth, who now reigns on high not only in splendor and glory but also in love and compassion.

Jesus presents an evocative image of rest and a redefined, reimagined restfulness. This isn't mere cessation of labor but a profound integration into the rhythms of God's kingdom. When Jesus beckons the weary and burdened to come to him, he's not offering a temporary reprieve but an invitation to a transformative yoke. In the ancient world, a yoke symbolized servitude, but here, Jesus inverts it—his yoke is "easy," his burden "light." It suggests that the true rest we yearn for is found not in isolation or escape but in active partnership with him, learning the unforced rhythms of grace, where work and rest coalesce in a divine dance.

Finally, to behold the Son is to gaze upon the face of the Father, for in the Son, the Father's love, mercy, justice, and grace are made manifest. This dynamic revelation calls us not merely to understand but to participate, to be drawn into the eternal relationship that the Father shares with the Son.

Big Idea: Embrace Jesus's yoke of humility and service, finding rest in his teachings and love—while actively extending his peace and justice to the world.

Reflection: In what ways have you experienced or extended the rest that Jesus offers? How might you more deeply yoke yourself to Jesus's teachings, particularly in service and humility?

Prayer: Gracious Savior, amid our expectations, anxieties, and questions, anchor us in your unchanging love. May we be bearers of your yoke, reflecting your humility and grace, serving as conduits of your peace and justice. May we see an opportunity to extend your kingdom in every weary heart and burdened spirit. In your name, we pray. Amen.

Day 23

God Wants Mercy and Compassion, Not Rules

Reading: Matthew 12:1-21

Matthew 12:1-21 invites us into a life of mercy and compassion, demonstrating the grand design of God's kingdom—a realm soaked in God's love, peace, goodness, justice, and hope.

As we delve into these verses, the Pharisees confront Jesus for apparently breaking the Sabbath by permitting his disciples to pluck grain. In their eyes, this was labor—a direct violation of the Torah (the first five books of the Hebrew Bible).

However, Jesus, recalling the example of David, redirects their attention from legalism to the spirit of the Scriptures. The more profound mystery here isn't about grain or the Sabbath. It's about understanding that God inspired the Scriptures to serve humanity, not enslave people. The Son of Man, Jesus asserts, is the true Lord of the Sabbath and, by extension, the Lord of the holy Scriptures and all humanity and creation.

In our spiritual journey, this chapter prompts us to reflect on how we might sometimes become like the Pharisees—caught in self-made spiritual regulations, losing sight of mercy's weightier call. How often do we prioritize rituals, missing out on opportunities for compassion and service to others? But how does God want us to act? "I desire mercy, not sacrifice."

The episode with the man with the withered hand is particularly illuminating. The Pharisees question Jesus, testing the waters, seeing if he would heal on the Sabbath. In response, Jesus restores the man's hand, displaying a grander vision of love and justice. We fulfill the Bible's commands not by strict adherence but by active compassion, pointing to the kind of justice that recognizes the inherent worth of every individual.

In this narrative, Jesus reveals himself as the promised servant of Isaiah and as the embodiment of God's justice, mercy, and reconciling mission. "In his name, the nations will put their hope."

For in Jesus, we find the model of humility, service, and radical love. As we look to him, we find our compass recalibrated—away from self-preservation towards other-centered service, away from mere piety towards compassion, away from despair to hope. Through Jesus, we discover the grace that empowers us to be disciples, addressing societal ills with courage, compassion, and conviction. Through Jesus's power and grace, we proclaim a kingdom where the blind see, the oppressed are free, the wronged receive justice, and all humanity and creation celebrate Christ's victory, justice, compassion, shalom, and hope.

Big Idea: Embrace mercy and compassion over tradition, demonstrating Jesus's radical love in every relationship and interaction.

Reflection: In what areas have you prioritized religious tradition over compassion and love? How can you embody the radical love and service of Jesus in your interactions today?

Prayer: Lord Jesus, the Lord of the Sabbath, please teach us to see beyond mere rituals and embrace the more profound call to mercy and love. By your grace, equip us to be agents of peace, justice, and reconciliation in a broken world. In your name, we pray. Amen.

Day 24

Transformed Words, Actions, and Hearts

Reading: Matthew 12:22–50

As we delve into Matthew 12:22–50, we find ourselves confronted with a stunning mosaic of encounters, teachings, and rebukes, each fragment revealing a deeper facet of Jesus's mission and our call to discipleship.

This passage offers a poignant reminder: amid local and global strife and discord, a transformed heart is a beacon of hope. It calls believers to authentic relationships that transcend divisive narratives. Christ's teachings challenge us to replace conflict with kingdom-minded peacemaking and unity, making peace and reconciliation paramount in an oft-divided and war-torn world.

The opening scene unfurls with a demon-oppressed man being healed. Immediately, controversy ensues. Some marvel, while others accuse Jesus of drawing power from Beelzebub, the prince of demons. Christ's response is astute: "Every kingdom divided against itself is brought to desolation" (v. 25). A divided heart, community, or kingdom cannot stand. In our spiritual journey, we must be wary of such divisions. Are we sometimes guilty of letting bitterness, jealousy, or suspicion mar our understanding of God's works in others?

This narrative spirals into deeper layers with Jesus's chilling warning against the "unforgivable sin" of blasphemy against the Spirit. At its core, it's a call to recognize and honor God's work in the world and within us. Denying the evident move of the Spirit risks hardening one's heart to the point of spiritual numbness. Where is God bringing peace and light into the world, and how can we join in?

Jesus's teaching extends into the importance of words and actions, emphasizing their roots in the heart. "Out of the abundance of the heart, the mouth speaks" (v. 34). Our words and actions, in their authenticity, reveal our spiritual condition. Are our hearts brimming with grace, humility, and love for our neighbors and enemies alike? Do we genuinely serve others with compassion, or are we swayed by the tides of public opinion and self-interest?

As Jesus's family appears on the scene, he shifts our understanding of kinship. "Whoever does the will of my Father in heaven is my brother, sister, and mother." Here, we glimpse the nature of the kingdom—a community transcending biological ties united in a shared mission. This kingdom beckons us to a life characterized by justice, reconciliation, and unwavering witness to Jesus. The road may be challenging, but we're not alone. With his inexhaustible love and enabling grace, Christ empowers us to rise to this transformative call.

Big Idea: A transformed heart, brimming with Jesus's love, reshapes our words, actions, and relationships, calling us into a kingdom community that transcends worldly divisions.

Reflection: Where might we be harboring division in our hearts or communities, preventing us from fully recognizing God's works? How do our words and actions reflect the state of our hearts?

Prayer: Lord Jesus, help us discern your Spirit's movements in our midst. Fill our hearts with love, humility, and grace so that we might be faithful witnesses to your kingdom. Draw us into a deeper fellowship with you, enabling us to serve with compassion, seeking justice, and walking humbly in your ways. Amen.

Day 25

Soils of the Heart

Reading: Matthew 13:1-23

In the thirteenth chapter of Matthew's Gospel, we read a profound parable—the parable of the sower. When the sower scatters seeds, they land on various grounds: some on the path, some on rocky places, some among thorns, and others on good soil. These soils stand as metaphors for the receptivity of our hearts to God's word. The hard path is the closed heart, the rocky ground is the surface-deep heart, the thorny ground is the distracted heart, and the good soil is the receptive and fruitful heart. These are the soils of the human heart.

It's easy to think of Christianity as a set of beliefs or behaviors, but Jesus says no—it's an agriculture of the soul. Jesus says we must prepare the soil of our hearts to receive God's word in a way that brings a harvest. What type of soil describes your heart? How are you receiving the word of God? Because in answering these questions, we are not merely identifying our spiritual condition. We are setting the course for our spiritual journey—toward or away from a harvest of the Spirit that could be extraordinarily abundant.

Here's the challenge: Are you ready to reflect honestly on the type of soil that currently describes your heart? Is it the hard path, resistant and closed off? Is it rocky ground, enthusiastic but lacking depth? Is it among thorns, crowded with competing concerns? Or is it good soil, receptive and fruitful? The wonder of the gospel is that we're not stuck with the soil we have. Through the grace of God, the Spirit's power, and intentional spiritual practices, we can cultivate our hearts into becoming that good, fruitful soil.

The world is watching. They're looking to see if our faith is genuine, if it produces something more than words, something that looks like Jesus—compassionate, just, loving, and good. They're desperate to see a faith that isn't just proclaimed but lived out, a gospel that is good news and fruit. Will we show them? Will our lives offer them a taste of the abundant harvest that God longs to bring forth, not just in us but also in them?

Big Idea: Cultivate receptive hearts to God's word, allowing it to transform our actions and relationships in Christ's love.

Reflection: Which soil type most closely resembles your heart today, and why? How might you cultivate a fertile heart receptive to God's word?

Prayer: Gracious Sower, thank you for sowing your word into our lives. Soften our hearts, make them receptive to your truth, and let us bear fruit that reflects your love and grace. In the mighty name of Jesus, we pray. Amen.

Day 26

Amid the Harvest

Reading: Matthew 13:24-58

The parables in Matthew 13:24-58 reveal the kingdom of heaven through the ordinary images of our world: seeds, yeast, treasure, fishing, and pearls. But these aren't just mere anecdotes; they're living allegories, echoing deeper truths about the kingdom, our hearts, and our mission.

In the parable of the weeds, we discern God's kingdom grows amid an intertwined realm of good and evil, righteous and unrighteous, just and unjust. Righteousness, justice, and peace grow amid the weeds of their opposites. In our passion for righteousness, we might be tempted to "weed out" the wrong, or, conversely, we may fail to see the fruit of where God is at work, growing fruit and a harvest amid the world's brokenness. But Jesus cautions patience. The harvest is his, and he will set things right in due time. This speaks volumes of reconciliation, patiently seeking peace and justice even when our world appears entangled in violence and chaos.

The yeast, while minuscule, influences the whole dough, reminding us of the transformative power of God's kingdom. Just as a tiny seed grows into a mammoth tree, a small act of compassion, humility, or justice can create ripples in the grand scheme. We're called not to underestimate our "small" roles in the expansive narrative of God's kingdom.

When we discover hidden treasures and pearls of great value, we experience the joy of encountering the kingdom. It's worth everything. The essence of the gospel is forsaking all else for the incomparable worth of knowing Jesus. It's about valuing Christ above all worldly treasures and, in that pursuit, finding true life. At the end of the age, Jesus will judge between the wicked and righteous, and the meaningless things of this world and true treasure. Our job is to become a disciple in the kingdom of heaven amid the harvest.

Many will dishonor Christ, but our role is to honor, glorify, and follow him, alerting people everywhere to the wheat, mustard seeds, yeast, hidden treasures, pearls, good fish, and harvest all around us—signs of the kingdom of heaven. Jesus's love and grace empower us to be agents of peace, channels of justice, and bearers of the good news.

Big Idea: Embrace the small yet transformative acts of love and justice in daily life, trusting God's timing and valuing his kingdom above all.

Reflection: How are you waiting for God's timing? What small act of love or justice can you commit to today, trusting in its ripple effect for God's kingdom?

Prayer: Gracious Lord, help us discern the depth of your kingdom narratives in our lives. Amid the intertwined complexities of life, may we rest in your perfect judgment. Let us value your kingdom above all else, recognizing the worth of your grace. Empower us, Lord, to be vessels of your peace, humility, and love. In Jesus's name, amen.

Day 27

The Cost and Call of Kingdom Life

Reading: Matthew 14:1–12

Matthew 14:1–12 presents the harrowing tale of John the Baptist's death. It's a tragic account of the confrontation between the kingdom of Herod and the kingdom of God. At first glance, it's a story of power, politics, and a beheading. Yet, underneath, it's a narrative of courage, witness, and the cost of discipleship.

John the Baptist took center stage in the vast theater of life, unwaveringly proclaiming God's justice. His voice echoed in the corridors of power, confronting Herod's sin. He wasn't silenced by the palace's gilded halls nor swayed by the allure of political expediency. Instead, he exemplified the audacity of speaking truth in a world that often rewards lies. He witnessed to a reality larger, more vibrant, and more genuine than the courts of Herod.

This isn't merely an ancient story. The call of John reverberates in our spiritual lives. Like John, the Spirit beckons us to bear witness to a kingdom not of this world but for this world. This involves embracing a countercultural narrative that sees the world not as a competitive arena but God's good creation, awaiting renewal and reconciliation.

The kingdom John proclaimed and Jesus embodied urges us towards radical discipleship. This isn't about simple moralism but about a transformative way of life. It's about love that transcends boundaries, humility that kneels to wash feet, peace that seeks justice, compassion that embraces the marginalized, and hope that stares down the face of death.

John's martyrdom reminds us of the cost of this discipleship. To follow Jesus might lead us into places of discomfort, even confrontation. Yet, as those enveloped by the love and grace of Jesus, we are not left to our devices. The Jesus who walked on water, fed thousands, performed miracles, and rose from the dead is the same Jesus who empowers us to live out these values of the kingdom of heaven. His grace is our bedrock, His love our guiding compass.

How, then, should we live? We start by cultivating habits that root us deeply in God's kingdom. We recognize that reconciliation is the heart of the gospel, that enemies can become neighbors, and that service is the tune to which kingdom dancers move.

Big Idea: Bear witness to God's upside-down kingdom with courageous love, even amid worldly power structures.

Reflection: Where are we being called to bear witness to God's kingdom amid worldly power structures? In what areas of our life is the cost of discipleship challenging us to rely more deeply on the grace of Jesus? The story of John the Baptist shows that following Jesus may cost us everything. Are we willing to pay whatever price comes our way as Christ's disciples?

Prayer: Heavenly Father, amid the clamor of worldly kingdoms, tune our hearts to the rhythm of your kingdom. May we bear witness to your truth, love, and justice, even when the cost is high. Empower us, sustain us, and guide us. In Jesus's name. Amen.

Day 28

Journeying Beyond Our Expectations

Reading: Matthew 14:13-36

Matthew 14:13-36 is a rich tapestry of Jesus's power and compassion, interwoven with the very human reactions of his disciples. As Jesus feeds the five thousand and walks on water, we're given a glimpse into the expansive nature of God's kingdom and heart for humanity.

To begin, we see Jesus withdrawing to a desolate place upon hearing of John the Baptist's death. Grief, it seems, isn't alien to the Son of God. However, in his solitude, multitudes follow him, and instead of turning them away, Jesus heals their sick. His compassion interrupts his grief.

From five loaves and two fish, a feast emerges. Here, we see a God of abundance capable of multiplying our small offerings exponentially. It's a compelling picture of the way God's economics work. In a world driven by scarcity and hoarding, Jesus invites us into a rhythm of generosity, challenging us to believe that our "little" can achieve much in his hands.

The scene shifts from the miraculous feast to the water's tumultuous expanse. The disciples, facing a storm, are met with an incredible sight: Jesus walking on water. Peter's venture out of the boat symbolizes the audacious faith that's called from us. He succeeds briefly, then falters, yet Jesus reaches out to save us even in our doubts. This passage whispers to our souls, nudging us to step out in faith, even when the waves of life's uncertainties rage around us. If we falter, the outstretched hand of grace is always there.

The kingdom of God doesn't operate on the same principles as our world. It's a realm where humility, love, and radical faith are the order of the day. Jesus challenges us to love our neighbors and enemies with the same compassion he showed the crowds. He calls us to a life where we serve out of abundance, not scarcity, and we take steps of faith, not cower in fear.

The heartbeat of this narrative is Jesus. His love doesn't count the cost but gives freely. His enabling power beckons us to do the impossible. His grace catches us when we stumble.

Big Idea: Embrace Jesus's radical love, stepping out in faith and serving others with abundant compassion amid life's storms and scarcities.

Reflection: Where is Jesus inviting you to step out in faith, and what fears hold you back? How can you embody the kingdom's values of generosity and service in a world marked by scarcity and self-preservation?

Prayer: Lord Jesus, help us to see the world through your eyes of compassion and grace. Embolden us to step out, trusting in your enabling power. May we be conduits of your love, peace, and justice. Amen.

Day 29

Heart Over Hands

Reading: Matthew 15

Matthew 15 reveals a profound tension between outer form and inner substance. The Pharisees confront Jesus about his disciples not following tradition, specifically the ceremonial washing of hands. To this, Christ responds with a far-reaching truth: "The things which proceed out of the mouth come forth out of the heart . . . out of the heart come forth evil thoughts . . ." (vv. 18–19). Essentially, the heart's condition matters more than mere religious practices or ceremonial acts.

Dive deeper, and you'll realize this isn't just about washing hands. It's about the state of our hearts concerning the world and God's call on our lives. This theme continues as a Canaanite woman, considered an outsider, displays a faith that astonishes Jesus, leading to her daughter's healing. These two tales juxtaposed show a startling contrast. The religious elites miss the heart of the matter, while an outsider captures it. The question that surfaces is, where is our heart positioned?

Spiritually, we must resist the trap of elevating rituals, traditions, and appearances over genuine faith, love, and humility. External adherence to religious duties can become a facade, concealing a heart far from God. At the same time, a sincere heart, even from unexpected quarters, can find grace in God's eyes. It's not the rituals that define us but the relationship, not the ceremonies but compassion.

This chapter nudges us towards a reoriented life. Peace, reconciliation, and love aren't just ideals to strive for; they are outflows of a heart anchored in Jesus Christ. The call isn't simply to abstain from evil but to cultivate a heart that naturally flows towards justice, service, humility, and faith. In essence, our inner transformation leads to outer reformation.

The crux of this chapter leads us back to Jesus. He showcases a love that overlooks boundaries, as seen in feeding the four thousand, a predominantly gentile crowd. This radical inclusivity and grace remind us that Jesus's love and enabling power are available to all. Christ's ministry wasn't just about adhering to the law but unveiling the love behind it. As disciples, Jesus does not just call us to avoid wrongdoing; he empowers us by grace to radiate his love, humility, and compassion.

Big Idea: Anchor your actions in heart transformation, prioritizing genuine faith and compassion over mere ritual.

Reflection: Are we sometimes more focused on external religiosity than the condition of our heart? How can we cultivate a heart overflowing with genuine love, humility, and compassion?

Prayer: Lord Jesus, let our hearts be in sync with yours. May we value genuine faith over mere form. Teach us to love as you love, serve as you serve, and live as reflections of your grace. Amen.

Day 30

Seeking Signs and Discerning Yeast

Reading: Matthew 16:1–12

In the expanse of Matthew 16:1–12, there is a profoundly resonant moment where the Pharisees and Sadducees approach Jesus, demanding a sign from heaven. We might think our faith would be secure if only we had a sign! But they were still unsatisfied even in the face of his miraculous works. Jesus responds by pointing out their ability to interpret the skies for weather but their inability to discern the "signs of the times."

But it isn't merely about external signs; it's about the condition of our hearts. The demand for a sign shows a heart not attuned to God's ongoing work in the world, his new creation unfolding even amid the old. But isn't that our story, too? How often do we miss the manifestations of the kingdom of God around us because we're looking for something spectacular?

Immediately following this, Jesus warns his disciples about the "yeast" of the Pharisees and Sadducees. Just as a little yeast permeates and rises the entire dough, so too, unchecked, our spiritual blindness, pride, or hypocrisy can affect our entire being. This is not merely about doctrine but about our hearts' deep attitudes and postures.

What does this mean for our spiritual lives? Our efforts to love our neighbors and enemies, to proclaim the gospel, to serve others selflessly, or to witness Christ's transforming power all demand a heart untainted by self-righteousness or hypocrisy.

Moreover, the "yeast" of the world encourages us to seek validation through grand gestures and tangible achievements, yet the gospel whispers a counternarrative: that real transformation begins inwardly. Our commitment to justice, love, and humility directly results from our inner transformation by the grace and love of Jesus.

Our gaze should ultimately rest on Jesus, who didn't simply give a sign but became the Sign. His life, death, and resurrection are the most profound markers of God's love and redemption for humanity. As we navigate the tensions of this world, may we remember that it's through Christ's enabling and grace that we can genuinely discern, love, serve, and bear witness to him.

Big Idea: Cultivate an attentive heart to discern God's work in the world, resisting the lure of external validations and remaining rooted in Jesus's transformative love.

Reflection: In what areas of your life are you seeking signs instead of resting in the assurance of Christ's finished work? What "yeast" might subtly influence your heart, and how can you surrender it to Jesus?

Prayer: Lord Jesus, guide our hearts to discern the signs of your kingdom amid the clamor of this world. Please help us to recognize and resist the subtle influences that can lead us astray. Root us deeply in your love and grace so we might live as true reflections of your heart for the world. Amen.

Day 31

Discipleship's Deep Calling

Reading: Matthew 16:13-28

In Matthew 16:13-28, Jesus poses a question, resonating through the corridors of time: "Who do you say I am?" Instinctive and divinely revealed, Peter's response affirms Jesus as the Messiah. Yet, moments later, he's rebuked for his worldly understanding of the Messiah's mission. This duality of spiritual insight and human misconception encapsulates the constant tussle within our souls.

The heart of this passage centers on identity—both Jesus's and ours. By recognizing him as the Messiah, we also face our call to discipleship, which is neither glamorous nor straightforward. It demands self-denial and a willingness to embrace the cross, symbolizing the trials and tribulations we encounter in our faith journey.

However, this isn't a call to an ascetic or sorrow-laden life. It's an invitation to experience the authentic, abundant life Christ promises, found paradoxically when we lose our life for his sake. In laying down our self-centered ambitions, desires, and fears, we discover the profound peace, justice, truth, and reconciliation only Jesus offers.

Embracing this understanding of discipleship reshapes how we live. It steers us toward humility, acknowledging that our wisdom, apart from God, is flawed. It challenges us to live a life of love and service, not just to those we deem "lovable" but also to those we struggle to love. In this struggle, Jesus's love shines most brilliantly amid our imperfections. His love doesn't merely enable us to love others; it transforms our definition of love.

Furthermore, our commitment to the kingdom isn't merely a vocal proclamation of the gospel; it's a life that testifies to its transformative power. Every act of compassion, every call for justice, every instance of forgiving and seeking forgiveness, and every moment we choose to serve rather than be served, we echo Peter's confession and display who Jesus truly is to the world.

As we grapple with these profound truths, let us not forget that Christ's enabling grace empowers us. The journey of discipleship, while marked with challenges, is not lonely. Jesus, in his boundless love, walks alongside us, guiding, strengthening, and restoring.

Big Idea: Recognize Jesus as the Messiah and, in response, live a self-denying, love-filled life that testifies to his transformative power.

Reflection: In what areas of your life are you struggling to deny yourself and take up your cross? How might recognizing Jesus as the Messiah transform your daily interactions and priorities?

Prayer: Lord Jesus, in your profound love, you call us to a deep and transformative discipleship. Please help us to recognize you daily, to lay down our lives, and to live in the fullness of your grace. As we deny ourselves, may we find our true selves in you. Amen.

Day 32

From Mountain Peaks to Daily Streets

Reading: Matthew 17

In Matthew 17, we journey from the luminous peak of transfiguration to the everyday streets where faith feels diminutive, like a mustard seed. In the glow of the mountaintop, Jesus stands transformed, conversing with Moses and Elijah, revealing his divine nature and connection to God's redemptive plan. Yet, as they descend, the disciples confront their limitations in the face of a boy tormented by an evil spirit.

This juxtaposition of divine radiance and human frailty captures the essence of our spiritual journey. We often experience moments of spiritual clarity, where God's presence feels palpable, only to be followed by valleys of doubt and challenges.

But what does this chapter whisper into the depths of our souls? It beckons us to understand that the Christian journey isn't about perpetually residing on spiritual mountaintops. Instead, it's about carrying the transformative revelation of Jesus into our everyday lives. It's about recognizing that even faith as small as a mustard seed has immense power when anchored in Jesus Christ.

As disciples, the implications for how we live are profound. We're called to a life of humility, acknowledging our limitations while leaning into God's boundless strength. Such humility allows us to serve our neighbors, even our adversaries, with a love that transcends human comprehension. It's a love that seeks reconciliation, embodies justice, and communicates the gospel not just through words but, more vitally, through actions.

When confronted with the coin in the fish's mouth, Jesus, in his characteristic wisdom, communicates a nuanced understanding of freedom and responsibility. While he, the Son, owes nothing, he pays the temple tax to avoid offending. This narrative teaches us about living harmoniously within our communities, prioritizing peace, and always pointing to the higher kingdom values.

Throughout this chapter, the overwhelming love, grace, and enablement of Jesus shine resplendent. He doesn't scold the disciples for their lack of faith but encourages them towards a deeper trust. His patience and enduring commitment to their growth underscore how he mentors each of us, nurturing our faith, refining our understanding, and empowering our service.

Big Idea: Carry the revelation of Christ's divinity into daily life, trusting his grace to transform even our smallest faith into profound acts of love and service.

Reflection: How can you bring the revelation of Christ from your spiritual "mountaintop experiences" into your daily interactions? Where in your life is Jesus calling you to exercise faith, even if it feels as small as a mustard seed?

Prayer: Gracious Savior, in the ebb and flow of our faith journey, anchor us in your unchanging love. Empower us to live humbly, serve with love, and trust your ever-present grace, even when our faith wavers. May our lives continually point to you, the source of all hope and transformation. Amen.

Day 33

Childlike Heart, Endless Grace

Reading: Matthew 18

Matthew 18 dives deep into the nature of kingdom living. The disciples, consumed with hierarchical ambitions, ask, "Who is the greatest in the kingdom of heaven?" Jesus's response, showcasing a child, radically redefines greatness in his kingdom. It's a realm where humility reigns, the vulnerable are esteemed, and every wandering sheep matters to the Shepherd.

At the heart of this chapter lies a call to a transformative spiritual posture: becoming like a child. This doesn't denote naivety but a heart posture of humility, trust, and dependency. Children recognize their neediness; they don't boast about their self-sufficiency. Similarly, the kingdom invites us to acknowledge our dependency on God's grace.

Embracing such humility paves the way for a life echoing peace, justice, and reconciliation. The chapter speaks to dealing with conflicts within the community. It underscores the importance of genuine confrontation, always aimed at restoration. To live in the kingdom means to be agents of peace, not merely peacekeepers. It means actively working toward justice and reconciliation, even when uncomfortable.

The parable of the unmerciful servant further cements the centrality of grace and forgiveness in kingdom living. The vast debt forgiven by the king mirrors the immeasurable grace we've received in Christ. Yet, how often do we, like the servant, forget this grace and withhold forgiveness from those who owe us much less? Our call is to forgive, not from a reservoir of our strength, but from the overflow of grace we've experienced in Christ.

Jesus, throughout his ministry, modeled this radical, countercultural way of living. His love, grace, and humility were teachings and a way of life. Jesus invites us, empowers us, and graces us to walk in his footsteps. Every act of humility, every effort towards reconciliation, and every gesture of forgiveness testifies to the world the profound love of Jesus.

Big Idea: Embrace childlike humility and dependency on Jesus Christ, allowing his grace to fuel a life of reconciliation, justice, and boundless forgiveness.

Reflection: Where in your life is God calling you to embrace childlike humility and dependency? How might a deeper revelation of Jesus's grace towards you transform your ability to forgive others?

Prayer: Lord Jesus, draw us deeper into the heart of your kingdom, where humility and grace shine brightest. Transform our hearts to be like children, dependent and trusting. Empower us to pursue lives of reconciliation, justice, and boundless forgiveness, mirroring your endless love and grace. Amen.

Day 34

Prioritizing Kingdom Values

Reading: Matthew 19

Matthew 19 challenges conventional norms, shedding light on the values of the kingdom of heaven. From the sanctity of marriage to the weighty discourse on wealth, this chapter prompts profound reflection on our heart postures and priorities.

Jesus's teachings on marriage emphasize commitment and the original divine intent. Rather than getting caught in the minutiae of the law, Christ directs us back to God's original design, where two become one. It is a profound reminder that God's intentions always encompass depth, intimacy, and unwavering commitment.

In our journey through Matthew 19, it's crucial to pause and recognize the weight and pain that discussions on marriage might evoke, especially for those who've experienced its dissolution. Jesus speaks of God's original design for marriage, but we live in a broken world where relationships, like everything else, are affected by human frailty. If you've endured the heartache of a marriage ending, please know this: God's grace is bigger than any circumstance, and God's love for you remains steadfast. Jesus, who was well acquainted with sorrows, stands close to the brokenhearted. In him, there's healing, hope, and a new beginning. Remember, your identity is rooted not in marital status or past hurts but in Christ's all-encompassing love for you.

The next part of the chapter is the narrative of the rich young ruler. His earnest query, "What good thing must I do to get eternal life?" reflects a more profound, universal longing. Yet, Christ's challenge—to sell all he had—revealed the true anchor of the ruler's heart. It wasn't the act of giving away riches but the unmasking of where his true devotion lay.

Wealth isn't evil. Yet, its grip on our hearts can be a hindrance. The ruler's sorrow-laden departure illustrates a truth: anything we place above God, be it wealth, relationships, or ambitions, can deter us from fully experiencing kingdom life. The profoundness is encapsulated in Jesus's words, "With humans this is impossible, but with God all things are possible." Our ability to prioritize the kingdom isn't self-manufactured but divinely enabled.

As disciples, this chapter calls us to a life marked by profound love, justice, humility, and service. Our allegiances, possessions, and desires ought to reflect kingdom values. Wealth, rather than being hoarded, should be leveraged for justice, compassion, and the service of others. Relationships should mirror Christ's selfless love, commitment, and reconciliation.

It is Jesus, in his infinite love and grace, who empowers such living. We embark on a transformative journey towards genuine discipleship by understanding his teachings and surrendering our desires. In the face of societal norms and pressures, Christ's love grounds us, and his grace enables us to walk the path less traveled.

Big Idea: Prioritize kingdom values in every aspect of life, allowing Christ's love and grace to shape our desires, relationships, and use of wealth.

Reflection: Where in your life might worldly values be overshadowing kingdom principles? How can you better leverage what you have, whether it's wealth, skills, or time, for the sake of the kingdom?

Prayer: Lord Jesus, guide our hearts to prioritize your kingdom over fleeting worldly allurements. Empower us with your grace to lead lives marked by love, humility, and sacrificial service. Please help us to see as you see and to value as you value. Amen.

Day 35

Embracing Generous Grace

Reading: Matthew 20:1-16

Matthew 20:1-16 portrays a compelling parable that may seem perplexing at first glance. A vineyard owner hires laborers at various daily intervals yet rewards each with the same wage. This depiction of God's kingdom flies in the face of our earthly notions of fairness.

Moreover, this parable hints at a broader narrative: God extending salvation and eternal life not just to Israel but to gentiles as well, based solely on God's extravagant, unmerited grace revealed in Christ.

It's essential to recognize that the story isn't about labor or rewards but a deep exploration of God's grace. The vineyard owner's actions demonstrate an equality that doesn't rely on human merit or duration of service. Instead, it's grounded in God's boundless generosity. The complaint of the early workers isn't necessarily about their pay but their perception of the owner's generosity towards the latecomers.

This narrative poses significant questions for our spiritual lives. Do we, at times, resemble the disgruntled workers, measuring our service and commitment against others, expecting more from God because we think we've done more? Such sentiments reveal a limited understanding of grace.

Jesus constantly challenges us to rise above conventional perspectives. In God's kingdom, it isn't about earning or deserving but receiving. Considering this, the calling for Christians becomes evident. Our lives should exude peace, humility, and relentless love for neighbors, strangers, and enemies. By understanding that all we have resulted from God's generous grace, we're stirred to lead lives marked by compassion, forgiveness, and profound service.

It's in Jesus that we find the perfect embodiment of this grace. His sacrifice wasn't contingent on our merit but sprang from an eternal well of love. In Christ, we find the strength to transcend societal norms, to love without condition, and to serve without expectation. His grace enables us to respond to the world, not with judgment but with the same generous spirit portrayed by the vineyard owner.

Big Idea: Live generously, reflecting God's boundless grace, without comparing or measuring our service against others.

Reflection: How might we sometimes resemble the early laborers, feeling entitled to God's blessings? How can we cultivate a heart posture that rejoices in God's generosity to others, even when it challenges our sense of fairness?

Prayer: Generous God, help us to grasp the depths of your grace. Remind us that all we have comes from your hand, not because we've earned it, but because of your unfathomable love. Teach us to live with the same generosity of spirit, seeing others through your eyes and loving without measure. In Jesus's name, we pray. Amen.

Day 36

The Way of the Upside-Down Kingdom

Reading: Matthew 20:17-34

As we delve into Matthew 20:17-34, a profound juxtaposition emerges. On one end, we find Jesus once more predicting his impending suffering and death. On the other, we witness the blind men receiving their sight and the mother of James and John asking for special positions of honor for her sons in Jesus's kingdom. But woven into these narratives are rich teachings that upend our human expectations.

At the heart of this passage, we encounter a counterintuitive message of the kingdom. While the world's kingdoms might equate greatness with power and prestige, Jesus redefines it as service: "Whoever wants to become great among you must be your servant" (v. 26). This reversal is radical and transformative. It confronts our innate desires for prominence and invites us into a dance of humility and selflessness.

What does this mean for our spiritual lives? Well, for one, it suggests that the journey toward greatness is not upward but downward. It's not in climbing but in stooping. This focus on humility and service is where Jesus stands as our ultimate exemplar. He who was in the form of God did not exploit his position but emptied himself, taking the form of a servant. If we seek spiritual maturity, we must recognize that we cultivate it in the soil of service, humility, and self-sacrifice.

This chapter beckons Christians to live as agents of peace, justice, and reconciliation. When we choose the path of humility and service, we break down barriers, dispel hostilities, and mend broken relationships. We become ambassadors of a kingdom marked by a love that turns enemies into neighbors. By exemplifying Christlike humility, we demonstrate the gospel in action, living out the virtues of compassion, forgiveness, and unwavering faith.

However, as with any Christian endeavor, we can't navigate this journey through sheer willpower or determination. We require the enabling love and grace of Jesus. It is he who equips us to live counterculturally. It is in him that we find the strength to serve when the world tells us to dominate, to humble ourselves when society says to promote self, and to love when the culture advocates animosity.

Big Idea: Embrace the journey of true greatness by choosing the path of humility, service, and Christlike love in every facet of life.

Reflection: In what areas of your life is God calling you to serve and demonstrate humility? How might embracing the way of servitude lead to deeper spiritual maturity and transformation?

Prayer: Heavenly Father, thank you for showing us the way of true greatness through Jesus, our Servant King. Empower us by your Spirit to walk in humility, to serve selflessly, and to shine brightly as witnesses of your upside-down kingdom. Amen.

Day 37

Triumph, Trees, and Temples

Reading: Matthew 21:1-27

When Jesus made his grand entrance into Jerusalem on a donkey, the scene was awash with the resounding cries of "Hosanna!" This exclamation wasn't a mere cheer but a profound plea, "Save, please!" It's a vivid canvas, illuminating the tension between messianic expectations and Jesus's vision of his kingdom.

The scene of Jesus riding into Jerusalem on a donkey paints an evocative image that challenges our notions of kingship, power, and victory. This was no conventional entrance for a king; it was countercultural and deeply symbolic. Moreover, this prophetic act, foretold in Zechariah 9:9, underscores Jesus as the fulfillment of ancient promises. He wasn't merely a king of the present but the anticipated Messiah of old, bridging God's eternal narrative.

The donkey ride isn't a trivial detail but a profound declaration. It challenges our worldly understanding of power and authority. Through this act, Jesus unveils a kingship marked by humility, fulfillment of prophecy, a transformative kingdom, and unparalleled accessibility. It's an invitation to recognize and align with a King whose reign breaks every mold yet mends every heart.

The spiritual lesson embedded within Jesus's choice to ride a donkey into Jerusalem is profound: true power and leadership are found not in dominance and grandeur but in humility, service, and proximity to those we lead. As followers of Christ, we are called to reorient our understanding of greatness. In a world that often equates strength with aggression and success with superiority, we are invited to embrace a counternarrative, where we find our worth in serving others, drawing near to the marginalized, and walking humbly in our daily lives. It's a call to embody Christlike leadership in every sphere, recognizing that genuine influence arises from a heart that serves, loves, and humbles itself.

Amid the public euphoria, Jesus took a detour to a fig tree. Hungry, he found it barren. Even though it wasn't the season for figs, this tree, with all its leafy pretense, held no sustenance. It's more than an anecdote about a tree; it's a spiritual allegory. We, too, can display an outward religiosity, replete with leafy fervor but devoid of genuine fruits. But it's the authenticity of our faith, the fruits of love, humility, and service that truly matter.

Jesus's actions in the temple further accentuate this motif. The temple was meant to be a house of prayer, a bridge between God and his people. Yet, it had been reduced to a marketplace. Jesus's righteous anger wasn't against the traders per se but against a religious system that had lost its essence: justice, peace, integrity, truth, and reconciliation. There's a prophetic message here: religion, when misused, can overshadow its very purpose, estranging us from genuine communion with God and others.

Big Idea: Live authentically, bearing fruits of faith, and transform outward religiosity into genuine reflections of God's heart.

Reflection: Does your life mirror the humility of Christ's entry on a donkey, the fig tree's barrenness, or the temple's commercialism?

Prayer: Gracious Lord, as we delve into the depths of Matthew 21, let it not be mere words but a mirror reflecting our hearts. May we be drawn closer to you, bearing fruits of righteousness, love, and humility. Through your grace, empower us to be bearers of justice, peace, and reconciliation in a world so deeply in need. In Jesus's name, we pray. Amen.

Day 38

Active Faith, Fruitful Obedience

Reading: Matthew 21:28-46

In Matthew 21:28-46, we encounter a parable and a prophecy, each a rich tapestry of grace and challenge woven with the threads of the kingdom's surprising nature. It begins with a father asking two sons to work in his vineyard. One son initially refuses but later goes, while the other agrees to go but does not. Here, we see a picture of obedience transcending mere words; it's about the transformation of the heart that leads to action. This passage strips bare the illusion that verbal assent to God's call is equivalent to faithfulness.

For our spiritual lives, this parable acts as a mirror, reflecting the often discomforting truth that the kingdom of God is not affirmed by lip service but by living service. It is in the doing, the going, the being—embodied faith—that we truly honor our Father. This is an invitation to a spirituality that is active, responsive, and authentic, one that seeks peace and justice not as abstract concepts but as daily practices.

Moreover, this narrative calls Christians to a radical form of discipleship. It is one thing to love in word, and another to love in deed—especially when that love extends to neighbors and enemies alike. Our daily lives ought to be marked by the stones of reconciliation and the mortar of compassion. In the tumult of the vineyard—our world—we are beckoned to cultivate forgiveness and nurture faith through our presence and actions.

Yet, the chapter pushes us further into the prophetic, revealing that the stone the builders rejected has become the cornerstone. This stone, Jesus, exemplifies humility and service, even as he is destined to cause a falling and a rising of many. His life and message are the very embodiment of the gospel—the good news that is as much an offense to the self-righteous as it is a comfort to the repentant.

Considering these truths, how then shall we live? We are to be people whose lives testify to the enabling grace of Jesus—people who not only hear his words but become living epistles of his love and grace. To follow Jesus is to walk in the way of the son who, though initially resistant, chose obedience and thus honored his father.

Big Idea: Embody authentic discipleship by aligning actions with professed faith through Christ's enabling grace.

Reflection: Is there an area of your life where your actions have not aligned with your spoken commitments to God? How can the enabling love and grace of Jesus move you from inertia to action, from saying to doing, in your journey of discipleship?

Prayer: Lord of the Vineyard, who calls us to work in your fields, instill in us a spirit of faithful obedience and a heart that reflects your love. May your grace enable us to be disciples who not only hear but do, who not only speak of love but demonstrate it in our lives. In the name of Jesus, our cornerstone, we pray. Amen.

Day 39

Dressed for the Banquet

Reading: Matthew 22

In Matthew 22, we witness a mosaic of stories and teachings that reflect the profound dimensions of God's kingdom and the expectations laid upon its citizens. It begins with the parable of the wedding banquet, depicting divine generosity and the tragedy of human indifference. The kingdom of heaven, akin to a king who invites guests to the marriage feast of his son, confronts us with a gracious invitation. Yet, how often are we among those who ignore the call, busied by the concerns and desires of our daily preoccupations?

This chapter challenges us to examine our response to God's summons. Are we adorned in the wedding garments of righteousness, or are we scrambling in the alleyways of complacency? In essence, the parable isn't merely about accepting an invitation but about being properly attired for the occasion—dressed in the love, peace, justice, and humility that befit kingdom dwellers.

As the narrative unfolds, Jesus navigates a minefield of trick questions about taxes, resurrection, and the greatest commandment. His wisdom silences the cunning and reveals a life patterned after divine priorities. When quizzed about Caesar and God, Jesus offers an iconic answer: "Give therefore to Caesar the things that are Caesar's, and to God the things that are God's" (v. 21). Our lives are to be stamped with the image of God, as the coin bears the emperor's image, living in service to the Divine, even as we fulfill our earthly duties.

In a piercing synthesis of the law, Jesus distills our purpose into a dual love: for God and neighbor, seamlessly weaving them together. Here, love is not a nebulous sentiment but an active commitment, shaping our interactions, fueling forgiveness, and prompting service. This love does not discriminate between neighbor and enemy; it beckons us to a higher plane where love is our origin and destination.

Furthermore, we cannot disentangle this love from the story of Jesus himself, the cornerstone of faith. The christological conundrum he presents, "Whose son is the Christ?" leads us to the inescapable conclusion that Jesus is Lord, not merely David's son but his Lord. He calls for an allegiance that transcends familial and cultural ties, inviting us to a transformed identity rooted and grounded in his love.

So, how does this text sculpt our daily living? It carves out a place for peacemaking, for it is the peacemakers who are clothed in the righteousness of the kingdom. It underlines justice, as love seeks equitable treatment for all God's image bearers. It champions reconciliation, where the currency of forgiveness is more potent than Caesar's. It delineates a lifestyle of gospel communication, where actions resonate with the harmonic frequencies of Jesus's love.

Big Idea: Embrace God's invitation with a life adorned in Christlike love, actively pursuing righteousness, justice, and reconciliation.

Reflection: How are you responding to the invitation of God's kingdom? Are your garments reflective of the righteousness and love of Christ? In your daily dealings, how do you balance earthly responsibilities with heavenly allegiance?

Prayer: Lord of the Feast, clothe us in your righteousness that we may joyfully partake in your banquet. Grant us wisdom to navigate the complex currencies of this world while investing deeply in your kingdom. May love be our guide and your son, Jesus, our constant reference point. Amen.

Day 40

Authentic Greatness

Reading: Matthew 23

In Matthew 23, we are met with a sobering discourse as Jesus admonishes the religious leaders for their hypocrisy. With poignant clarity, he exposes the gulf between their teachings and actions, between the appearance of holiness and the heart of it. This chapter is a clarion call to self-examination and authenticity in our faith journey.

The biblical meaning here is multilayered; it is a critique of spiritual pride and a blueprint for genuine discipleship. Christ is not merely rebuking the Pharisees of old; he speaks across the centuries to any who would wear righteousness as a garment rather than a transformed nature.

Jesus beckons us into a deeper spiritual authenticity. The pitfalls Jesus identifies—the pursuit of honor, the burdening of others, the minutiae of law over the magnitude of love—are as relevant now as they were then. The chapter summons us to a discipleship of the heart, where our inner lives mirror our outer professions of faith.

But how should we then live? The way of Jesus outlined here is one of humility, service, and love. It is a journey marked by the washing of feet rather than the seeking of titles. It is to show compassion over compliance, to value justice over just appearances, and to prioritize reconciliation over regulation. Jesus urges us to be practitioners of faith, not just preachers of it, to embody grace so that our lives point, with humility, to Jesus Christ.

Jesus's pronouncement, the person "who is greatest among you will be your servant" (v. 11), inverts worldly paradigms of greatness, offering a kingdom where service is the hallmark of nobility. It is in the lowly act of service that we find the greatest expression of divine love. In this humble posture, we witness to Jesus most compellingly.

This chapter does more than point to Jesus; it throws us onto the grace of his example. We are called not to a life of self-generated piety but to one empowered by the love and grace of Christ Jesus himself. Our ability to live out the true spirit of the law, to show mercy and justice, and to walk humbly with our God stems from his enabling grace.

Big Idea: Live authentically in humility and service, reflecting the servant heart of Jesus in every aspect of life.

Reflection: Where might you value appearance over authenticity in your spiritual walk? How can your life better reflect the servant leadership exemplified by Jesus?

Prayer: Gracious Lord, search our hearts and strip away any facade of feigned righteousness. Cultivate in us a spirit of humility and service that honors you. Empower us by your grace to live authentically, love deeply, and serve faithfully, following the footsteps of Jesus, our ultimate guide and Savior. Amen.

Day 41

Anchored in the Awaited Dawn

Reading: Matthew 24:1–35

In Matthew 24:1–35, Jesus dismantles the disciples' traditional conceptions of permanence and stability. The temple, a symbol of certainty, will be undone, brick by brick. Herein lies a profound spiritual implication: what we often consider fixed and secure in our lives may not be so. The truest anchor must be found elsewhere.

Jesus speaks of false prophets, wars, natural disasters, and persecution. These events, while tumultuous, are not cues for us to unravel in despair but are instead signposts on the journey, calling us to deeper faith and dependence on God. Our spiritual lives are to be marked by watchfulness, an active waiting rooted in the practices of peace, justice, and reconciliation. It's not a call to a passive observance but to a vibrant and transformative engagement with the world.

This passage is also a call to repentance when the Spirit shows us that our attitudes, values, or allegiances have supported the hostilities, principalities, and powers of this world instead of the peace, justice, and reconciliation of Jesus Christ. Our loyalty must be to Jesus and his way of peace, truthfulness, reconciliation, justice, love, forgiveness, and compassion as we await his coming in all his splendor and glory.

In a world bristling with hostility, it is easy to respond in kind. Yet, the call of Jesus in this chapter is antithetical to the ethos of retaliation. To love our neighbors and, more radically, our enemies requires a counterintuitive strength that only Christ's love can engender within us. This love fuels our service to others, not as a burdensome duty but as the joyful outpouring of a life touched by divine grace. In the face of deception and false prophecies, we hold fast to truth, not as a weapon to bludgeon but as a balm to heal.

But none of this—our watching, repenting, loving, serving, or witnessing—is possible in our strength. The enabling grace of Jesus is essential to Christian discipleship. It is this grace that allows us to stand in the face of future uncertainty and present trials, not as those unmoored by the winds of change but as those anchored firmly in the hope of Christ's return.

Big Idea: Embrace active watchfulness in faith, embodying Christ's love and peace as we anticipate his return amid life's pain and uncertainties.

Reflection: How might our lives look different if we lived with the acute awareness of Christ's return? How does this passage call us to reshape our priorities and relationships?

Prayer: Lord of History, as we contemplate the unfolding of your story, grant us the wisdom to discern your hand at work amid the trials and tribulations of our times. May we hold loosely to the things of this world, instead securing our grip on the eternal hope offered in your Son. Teach us to love fiercely, serve selflessly, and communicate your gospel with urgency and compassion. In the assurance of your return, let us live each day with purpose, guided by your Spirit, until we see you face to face. Amen.

Day 42

Living the Now Until the Not Yet

Reading: Matthew 24:36–51

In this passage, Jesus speaks of the unknown hour, drawing us into the heart of divine mystery and reminding us that the precise moment of his return is veiled even from the angels. Jesus invites us to live in a spiritual tension between the now and not yet, between active waiting and holy living. Christ speaks to the core of our spiritual lives, where the uncertainty of the "when" leads us to the certainty of the "what"—that is, what we are called to do while we wait. The servant who is found faithful is the one who is actively engaged in their master's work, not the one idly watching the clock.

For Christians, this chapter calls us to a lifestyle that reflects the values of the kingdom we await. Christ beckons us toward peace and justice, not as distant concepts but as present realities we're to embody in our daily walk. The watchful servant is also the working servant, engaged in the ministry of reconciliation, sowing the seeds of the gospel in the fabric of everyday life.

In the fabric of these verses, Jesus reminds us that to follow him is to live out the paradox of the gospel: we love not only our neighbors but also our enemies; we serve others before ourselves; we hold faith as the bedrock of our actions; and we embrace compassion and forgiveness as our garments. The readiness Jesus speaks of is a readiness to live this out with humility that understands the hour of our calling is always now.

We are not just to wait for Christ but to walk as he walked. His love is the empowerment for our service, his grace the foundation for our forgiveness, and his life the blueprint for our own. The beauty of the gospel is that in his coming, Jesus inaugurated the kingdom, and in his return, he will complete it. Until then, our lives are to testify to the love and redemption Jesus offers.

Big Idea: Christians are called to actively manifest God's kingdom in the present by living lives of readiness through service, love, and peacemaking as we anticipate Christ's return.

Reflection: How are we manifesting the kingdom of God in our everyday lives? Are we the faithful servants, attentive to the needs of our Master's household, or are we the complacent ones, surprised by the Master's return?

Prayer: Lord of the Harvest, you have sown us into the world as emblems of your love and heralds of your peace. Grant us the grace to live expectantly, not with a passive gaze toward the skies, but with hands ready to serve, hearts ready to love, and feet ready to walk in your ways. May our lives be a continuous echo of your justice, compassion, and humility as we await your glorious return. Amen.

Day 43

Lamps Lit, Talents Spent, Hearts Open

Reading: Matthew 25

In the Gospel of Matthew, the twenty-fifth chapter is a triptych, displaying three profound spiritual scenes: the parable of the ten virgins, the parable of the talents, and the judgment of the nations. This passage beckons us into a kingdom ethic that transcends mere moralism and invites us into the transformative embrace of kingdom readiness, responsibility, and responsiveness.

Firstly, we witness the wise and foolish virgins. Here is a clarion call to vigilant preparedness. The oil in their lamps—could it not symbolize the Spirit's indwelling, a heart aflame with divine love and expectancy? As spiritual sojourners, we are urged to live in the active anticipation of Christ's return, not as a distant doctrine but as a present reality shaping every moment.

The parable of the talents follows, not merely a lesson in stewardship but a narrative that unfolds the risk of faith. To bury a talent is to shackle oneself to the fear of failure. Yet, the kingdom invites us into the daring adventure of faith. To invest what we have been given is to trust in the One who entrusts us. It is in this active engagement with the gifts we've received that our spiritual lives are most vividly expressed.

As the chapter concludes with the judgment of the nations, we see the kingdom's ethics fully displayed: the King identifies himself with the least of these. The spiritual life is not lived in abstract contemplation but in concrete acts of mercy, justice, and compassion. To serve the least is to serve Christ himself. The call is unequivocal: embody the love of Christ by extending justice, hospitality, service, and compassion impartially to all—and especially to those church and society consider the "least of these."

These parables are not mere moral injunctions but signposts pointing us to Jesus, in whom we find the love that fuels our lamps, the grace that emboldens us to invest our talents, and the mercy that moves us to see him in the faces of those in need. In Jesus, we know the love that compels us to a life of courage, character, and compassion.

But how does this translate to our daily walk? It means to live with purpose and passion, mindful that each day is a canvas for kingdom living. It means to pursue peace by being makers of peace, to enact justice by advocating for the oppressed, and to foster reconciliation by bridging divides with the love of Christ. It means that our faith is never private but profoundly public, a beacon of hope in a world that languishes in despair.

Big Idea: Actively demonstrate your readiness for Christ's return through vigilant faith, compassionate service, and courageous stewardship in everyday life.

Reflection: How are you keeping your lamp filled with the oil of God's Spirit? What has God entrusted you, and how are you investing it in his kingdom?

Prayer: Divine Shepherd, who calls us to readiness, responsibility, and responsiveness, let the light of your Spirit guide us to live expectantly, invest courageously, and love radically. May our lives reflect your kingdom's beauty, and our actions bear the imprint of your grace. In the name of Jesus, the first and the last, amen.

Day 44

The Blueprint of Sacrificial Love

Reading: Matthew 26:1–35

In Matthew 26, we are silent observers of a prelude to the crucifixion, unveiling human frailty juxtaposed against divine resolve. Here, the narrative weaves a tapestry of betrayal, anguish, and impending sacrifice—a tableau of the gospel itself.

The chapter opens with Christ's poignant awareness of his approaching death, a sacrificial lamb fully conscious of the altar before him. The anointing at Bethany is rich in symbolism; the costly perfume, a metaphor for the lavish love of God, poured out on humanity in the form of Christ's own life. The disciples' indignation mirrors our discomfort with such extravagant love and our tendency to misconstrue value with price tags rather than divine currency.

Judas's betrayal highlights a stark dichotomy within the human heart—our capacity for loyalty and our propensity for treachery. His actions prompt us to examine the devotion of our hearts. How often do we trade Jesus for lesser things? Yet, the narrative does not permit us to linger long in judgment; instead, it calls us into introspection and repentance.

The Last Supper is a poignant reminder of the new covenant, a promise embedded within the shared bread and wine, symbols of body and blood offered for the redemption of many. In this sacred moment, Jesus redefines community, service, and sacrifice. His directive to "do this in remembrance of me" is not merely a call to ritual but to a way of living marked by love, humility, and the rhythm of grace.

Juxtaposed with Jesus's steadfast love, Peter's forthcoming denial exemplifies the paradox of the human condition: our often faltering faithfulness met by God's unwavering commitment. This scene calls us to reflect on the nature of our discipleship. In our own strength, we are as fragile as Peter, yet in Christ, we find the grace to stand again, follow more closely, and witness more boldly.

In these verses, Jesus's steadfast march toward the cross beckons us to a life of humility, sacrifice, love, and dedication to God's will. Jesus's journey compels us to embrace the gospel's costliness and acknowledge that God's transformative work within us—and within creation—demands our wholehearted response. We are to be agents of forgiveness, bearers of peace, proclaimers of the gospel, and messengers of a love that reconciles and restores.

Big Idea: Embrace Christ's example of sacrificial love as the blueprint for our daily walk of faith, service, and witness.

Reflection: How is the costly perfume of our devotion being poured out in service to others? Are we prepared to face our moments of denial with the assurance of Christ's grace?

Prayer: Gracious Lord Jesus, as we reflect on your journey to the cross, embolden our hearts to live in the fullness of your love. Please help us be vessels of your peace, agents of your justice, and gospel ambassadors. May your unwavering love transform us as we seek to follow you in all things. Amen.

Day 45

Strength in Surrender

Reading: Matthew 26:36-46

In the shadowed grove of Gethsemane, we read a story that is as complex as it is intimate. Here, Jesus invites us into the depths of human vulnerability and divine mystery. This moment shrouded in night, unveils profound truths about the nature of God's kingdom and beckons us to live in a manner that reflects its values.

Firstly, this passage reveals the paradox of divine strength found in human weakness. Jesus, fully aware of the impending suffering, does not stoically dismiss his emotions but rather engages deeply with them, inviting his closest followers to watch and pray. In his plea, "My Father, if it is possible, let this cup pass away from me; nevertheless, not what I want, but what you want" (v. 39), we encounter a Messiah who embodies the fullness of humanity, including its anguish.

Spiritually, this teaches us that the journey of faith is not an escape from emotional turmoil but a path through it, with a posture of surrender. The scene at Gethsemane illustrates that in moments of our deepest despair, we are not to shun vulnerability but to embrace it as a place where grace can work profoundly.

As for how Christians should live, Gethsemane's echo reverberates through the ages, calling for a discipleship marked by a commitment to prayerful vigilance and the courage to confront the darkness, both within and without. Here, we learn that pursuing peace and justice begins with a heart attuned to the divine will, even when it leads to personal sacrifice.

Moreover, this passage invites us to consider our response to betrayal and suffering. Jesus, even in the shadow of betrayal, moves toward sacrificial love and redemption. His example challenges us to live out reconciliation, extend forgiveness to those who wrong us, and be agents of peace in a world of strife.

This humility—kenosis or self-emptying—is the cornerstone of engaging with others, serving without the need for recognition or reward. It is a radical call to love our neighbors and our enemies and testify to Jesus's reconciling work through acts of compassion and service.

This essence is encapsulated in Jesus's resolute statement, "nevertheless, not what I want, but what you want." It speaks of a discipleship undergirded by a trust that, even in suffering, God is working his purposes out. This trust enables us to follow Jesus, not as passive bystanders but as active participants in the unfolding story of God's redemptive plan.

Big Idea: Embrace vulnerability as a divine strength to live out sacrificial love and align with God's will.

Reflection: How can we embody a posture of surrender in our spiritual walks, especially in times of distress? In what ways are we being called to watch and pray in our current life circumstances?

Prayer: Heavenly Father, in the stillness of our souls, we seek the strength to embrace the cup you have set before us. Like your Son, may we find the courage to say, "Not what I want, but what you want." Grant us the grace to lead lives marked by prayer, humility, and sacrificial love. In Jesus's name, amen.

Day 46

Beyond Betrayal

Reading: Matthew 26:47-75

In the early morning's chill, beneath the olive trees' wavering shadows, Matthew 26:47-75 unfolds a narrative that arrests the heart. It presents a story of betrayal, denial, and the steadfast love of Jesus, weaving a lesson that resonates deeply within the Christian soul.

The biblical narrative captures the stark contrast between human frailty and divine fidelity. Judas's betrayal with a kiss juxtaposes the cowardice of friends with the courage of the Savior. Peter's denial, a thrice-repeated echo in the night, manifests the trembling weakness of even the most passionate followers. Yet, it is Jesus, amid false witnesses and the foreboding hum of impending suffering, who remains resolute, a beacon of truth and love.

This passage serves as a mirror for our spiritual lives, reflecting our tendencies to falter under pressure, betray with a kiss, or deny with a word. It reveals the fickle nature of our devotion, often swayed by fear or self-preservation. Yet, it also affirms that our failings are not the final word, for in the narrative, we find Jesus standing firm, a testament to the grace that outstretches our shortcomings.

This chapter informs us how to live by illustrating the stark difference between human and divine responses to adversity.

While betrayal and denial mar the pages of this account, they are overshadowed by the unwavering commitment of Jesus to fulfill his redemptive mission. It beckons us to strive for a faith that does not waver, a love that does not falter, and a witness that does not fail, even when faced with the most significant trials.

Through the lens of this Scripture, we are invited to reflect Jesus's love in our interactions, showing grace where there is betrayal and offering forgiveness where there is denial. It is a poignant reminder to hold fast to what is good, just, and true, embodying the peace and reconciliation that Jesus exemplified even as he was led like a lamb to the slaughter.

Moreover, Matthew 26:47–75 points us to Jesus's example of divine love, enabling grace, and the power to be his disciples—disciples who are not defined by their failures but by the One they follow. In the moments of our deepest failings, his strength is made perfect, his love most apparent, and his grace most needed.

Big Idea: Transform personal failings into steppingstones for grace-filled discipleship and authentic testimony.

Reflection: Where have we echoed Peter's denial in our lives, and how can we move towards a faith that stands firm in the face of trial? How can the love and grace of Jesus empower us to live out the gospel with integrity and courage?

Prayer: Lord of Steadfast Love, we seek your strength and grace amid our frailties and failings. Help us to lead lives that mirror your truth, to love as you love, and to stand for justice and peace as you stand. Forgive us for our denials and betrayals and enable us to be faithful witnesses to your gospel. In Jesus's name, we pray, Amen.

Day 47

Grace in the Shadows

Reading: Matthew 27:1–31

In the heartrending account of Matthew 27:1–31, we encounter the unfolding of divine purpose through human injustice. The chapter lays bare the raw narrative of Jesus's condemnation, a portrayal of society's broken systems, and the contrast of divine sovereignty against human machinations.

The biblical meaning here is profound: it presents the Son of God, who stands silent before his accusers, embodying the paradox of divine power cloaked in human frailty. It is a scene that juxtaposes the crowd's fickleness with the fidelity of Christ, the injustice of the sentence with the justice of his mission, and the humiliation of the scourge with the honor of his sacrifice.

This passage acts as a clarion call for our spiritual lives to recognize and confront the injustices around us, knowing that our Savior is acquainted with suffering and systemic wrongs. It challenges us to live not as passive bystanders but as active agents of change, striving for justice and peace, grounded in the reality of the cross and the hope of the resurrection.

This chapter informs how Christians should live by providing a stark example of the cost of discipleship. It calls for humility in the face of ridicule, love that extends even to enemies, and service that looks like the one who "came not to be served, but to serve" (Matthew 20:28). It is a call to bear our crosses, to stand for truth, and to exhibit compassion even when the world shows cruelty.

Furthermore, Matthew 27:1–31 points us to Jesus's unwavering love and grace that underpin true discipleship. His silence in the face of false accusations and his dignity amid mockery speak of a love so profound that it absorbs hate and grace so powerful and transforms shame into glory. In following Jesus, we are empowered to respond to life's trials with a love that is not of this world.

Big Idea: Live with resilient grace, confronting injustice with Christ's silent strength and transformative love.

Reflection: How can we, as disciples of Christ, confront injustice with the same silent strength Jesus demonstrated? How does his example inspire us to live out the gospel in both word and deed?

Prayer: Gracious God, as we reflect on the suffering of your Son, instill in us a spirit of humility and service. May we seek justice, love mercy, and walk humbly with you, even amid trials. Empower us to live out your love, to carry our crosses with the grace you provide, and to extend forgiveness as you have forgiven us. Through the example of Christ, may we be witnesses to your enduring love and transforming power. Amen.

Day 48

The Transformative Power of the Cross

Reading: Matthew 27:32-66

In the somber narrative of Matthew 27:32-66, we find ourselves at the crux of the Christian faith, beholding the profound mystery of redemption and sacrifice. This passage is not merely a historical account; it is a mirror reflecting profound spiritual truths that resonate with the core of our being. More than that, the cross and resurrection of Jesus Christ are the defining moments in the history of humanity and the cosmos.

At the heart of this passage is the crucifixion of Jesus. Here, the intersection of divine love and human suffering is laid bare. The cross, an emblem of agony and shame, paradoxically becomes the ultimate expression of God's love and grace. In Jesus's unjust suffering and death, we see the depth of human sin and the height of divine love. The cross is a stark reminder of the cost of our redemption, a price paid not in gold or silver but in the precious blood of Christ.

The cross of Christ symbolizes the holiness, mercy, love, freedom, healing, and power of God offered to a world soaked in bondage, suffering, sin, and evil. The cross is God's stunning act of love, word of hope, and offer of salvation to the world.

This chapter, however, is not only about the crucifixion; it's about the profound implications the cross holds for our spiritual lives. It calls us to a life of humility and self-denial, following the example of Christ who, "being in very nature God, did not consider equality with God something to be used to his advantage" (Phil 2:6, NIV). In a world that often values power and success, the cross challenges us to embrace vulnerability and sacrificial love.

Moreover, Matthew 27 speaks to the heart of Christian ethics. Jesus's silence in the face of false accusations, his forgiveness towards those who crucified him, and his commitment to God's will even unto death set a profound example for how Christians should live. This passage calls us to be agents of humility, peace, justice, and reconciliation in a world torn by strife and conflict. It challenges us to love our neighbors and enemies, serve others selflessly, and proclaim the gospel's transforming power.

The narrative also invites us to ponder the nature of true power and authority. The power of God, as demonstrated in Jesus's resurrection, is not coercive but transformative, not dominating but liberating. It's a power that brings life out of death and hope out of despair. In this light, our call to follow Jesus is not a call to a life of ease but to a life of faithful witness in the face of suffering and adversity, empowered by his grace and love.

Big Idea: Embrace sacrificial love and humble service, reflecting Christ's selfless example on the cross.

Reflection: How does the story of Jesus's crucifixion and resurrection challenge my understanding of power, success, and victory? How can I embody Christ's sacrificial love in my relationships and interactions with others?

Prayer: Heavenly Father, in the shadow of the cross, teach us the true meaning of love, sacrifice, and victory. Help us follow in the footsteps of your Son, Jesus Christ, who humbled himself to death, even death on the cross. May your Spirit empower us to lead lives marked by humility, service, and faithful witness to your transformative power. In Jesus's name, amen.

Day 49

Resurrection: A Call to Transformation

Reading: Matthew 28:1-15

In Matthew 28:1-15, we witness the dawning of a new era: the resurrection of Jesus Christ. This pivotal moment in history is not just a miraculous event but a profound message about the power of God, the defeat of death, and the birth of new hope.

The resurrection is the cornerstone of the Christian faith, symbolizing the triumph over death and the promise of new life in Christ. It declares that in Jesus, the finality of death is broken, giving way to eternal life. This truth is central to our spiritual lives, offering hope and meaning amid a world often clouded by despair and suffering.

This chapter goes beyond the mere fact of the resurrection; it also illuminates how we should live as followers of Christ. The women who first witnessed the empty tomb and encountered the risen Christ exemplify faith and courage. Despite their initial fear and uncertainty, they quickly act, obeying the angel's command to go and tell the disciples. Their response is a model for us: to act in faith, even when it means stepping into the unknown or facing our deepest fears.

In a broader sense, Matthew 28 challenges us to be messengers of this extraordinary news, embodying the hope and transformation it brings. It calls us to lead lives marked by the reality of the resurrection—lives of hope, courage, and new beginnings. The resurrection empowers us to approach our daily lives, relationships, and challenges with a perspective transformed by the knowledge that in Christ, death and despair do not have the final word.

This passage also speaks to skepticism and opposition to the gospel, as seen in the religious leaders' reaction and attempt to suppress the truth of the resurrection. It reminds us that the message of Jesus will often meet resistance, and yet, our call is to remain steadfast, anchored in the truth of the resurrection.

Reflecting on the resurrection reminds us of Jesus's love, enabling, and grace. Through his power, we can live out the kingdom's values: love, humility, service to others, compassion, and forgiveness. The resurrection assures us that his victory over sin and death undergirds our efforts in following and witnessing to Jesus.

Big Idea: Live boldly in the transformative hope of the resurrection, embodying its truth in every aspect of life.

Reflection: How does the reality of the resurrection shape my understanding of hope and new beginnings? How can I embody and communicate the transformative power of the resurrection in my life?

Prayer: Lord Jesus, in the light of your resurrection, renew our hearts and minds. Fill us with the hope and courage from your victory over death. Empower us to live as faithful witnesses of your resurrection, radiating your love and grace in all we do. In your name, amen.

Day 50

Living the Great Commission

Reading: Matthew 28:16-20

In the concluding verses of Matthew 28:16-20, often referred to as the Great Commission, we find the essence of our Christian calling. After his resurrection, Jesus gives his disciples a mandate that extends to all believers: to make disciples of all nations. This passage is not just an instruction; it is one of the foundations of our mission as followers of Christ.

The biblical meaning of this passage is profound. It marks the transition from Jesus's earthly ministry to the church joining with Christ in God's mission. The disciples are not just sent; they are empowered by Jesus's authority and promised his continual presence. This commissioning highlights the universal scope of the gospel, breaking down barriers and extending grace to every corner of the earth.

The Great Commission is a clarion call to active discipleship for our spiritual lives. It urges us to step beyond the comfort of familiar surroundings and engage with the world in a transformative way. Being a disciple of Christ means more than personal piety; it involves participating in God's mission to redeem and restore the world.

This passage informs how Christians should live in multiple profound ways. It calls us to embrace a life of truth-telling, gospel proclamation, peacemaking, justice-seeking, and reconciliation, reflecting the kingdom values Jesus preached. It emphasizes the importance of communicating the gospel in words and through actions that embody love, humility, and service. In a world often divided by cultural, ethnic, and religious lines, we call to bridge these divides, showing compassion and love even to those who may be considered our enemies.

Moreover, the Great Commission reinforces the importance of community and fellowship in our spiritual journey. Making disciples implies nurturing relationships, investing in others' growth, and building communities grounded in the love and teachings of Jesus. It also calls for a deep, abiding faith that trusts in Jesus's authority and his promise to be with us always.

In all this, the passage points us to Jesus—his love, enabling, and grace. It is by his strength, not ours, that we can fulfill this high calling. The Great Commission is not just a task to be accomplished; it's a journey to be lived out in the power and presence of Christ.

Big Idea: Embrace and live out the Great Commission with humble confidence and bold faith, knowing Jesus is with us always and extending Christ's love and teachings to all.

Reflection: How am I living out the Great Commission daily? How can I fully embrace the call to make disciples in my context?

Prayer: Lord Jesus, empower us to fulfill your Great Commission with courage and love. Help us embody your teachings and share your love with all we encounter. May we always be mindful of your presence with us, guiding and strengthening us for this sacred task. Amen.

Appendix 1

Daily Devotions with Jesus
Devotional Books and Podcast

DAILY DEVOTIONS WITH JESUS aims to help you dive deeply into the Bible, grow spiritually, and learn how to impact the world as a follower of Jesus Christ. After all, these devotions aren't just about learning about the Bible. They are also about growing ever more deeply in love with Jesus and following him with every fiber of your being and in every area of your life.

The Daily Devotions with Jesus devotional books and podcast offer a rich, engaging, and spiritually nourishing experience.

Podcast Links:

https://linktr.ee/dailydevotions
https://grahamjosephhill.com/devotions

Features:

The Daily Devotions with Jesus podcast offers a wide range of engaging and beneficial features:

1. **Daily Episodes:** Each episode, lasting 20–25 minutes, focuses on a specific Bible chapter or set of verses, offering a

detailed exploration (moving through the entire Bible, from Genesis to Revelation).

2. **In-Depth Reflections:** Rev. Dr. Hill provides insightful reflections and interpretations of each chapter or set of verses, helping you understand the context and relevance of the Bible in modern life.

3. **Historical and Cultural Insights:** The podcast provides background information on the historical and cultural context of the Bible passage to enhance your understanding.

4. **Christian Practices:** Each episode prompts you to reflect on how you can put the Bible's themes into practice through peacemaking, compassion, mercy, humility, love, justice, reconciliation, and more.

5. **Questions for Reflection:** The podcast offers questions for reflection and prompts for journaling to deepen your engagement with the Bible.

6. **Guided Prayers:** Each episode integrates guided prayers tailored to the day's Bible reading, encouraging spiritual growth and personal reflection.

7. **Flexible Pace:** The podcast offers relaxed and flexible pacing, allowing you to delve deeper into each chapter or set of verses.

8. **Devotional Books:** You can also get the devotional books accompanying this podcast, which are excellent for individual and group study (see https://grahamjosephhill.com/books).

9. **Bible Reading Plan:** You can follow the Bible Reading Plan at https://grahamjosephhill.com/biblereadingplan.

10. **Listening Options:** To listen on a range of podcasting platforms see https://linktr.ee/dailydevotions.

Appendix 2

Bible Reading Plan

GrahamJosephHill.com/BibleReadingPlan

This Bible Reading Plan shows you how to read the entire Bible in four to five years, exploring each chapter's themes in depth.

Each day you will read a chapter or set of verses and the devotional book dedicated to the book of the Bible you're reading and you can tune into the accompanying Daily Devotions with Jesus podcast episode.

Tips for Staying on Track:

1. Keep the Goal in Mind: The goal is to grow ever more deeply in love with Jesus and follow him with every fiber of your being and in every area of your life.

2. Set a Specific Time: Dedicate a specific time of the day to read and listen to the podcast episode.

3. Reflect and Pray: Take time to reflect on the chapter or set of verses and pray.

4. Keep a Journal: Note down your thoughts or insights from each day's reading.

5. Seek Understanding: If a chapter or set of verses are difficult to understand, consider consulting the Daily Devotions with Jesus devotional book dedicated to the book of the Bible you're reading.

6. Stay Committed: It's a long journey but staying committed will be rewarding.

7. Explore the Bible with Others: Discussing the Bible and devotions in groups can help keep you on track and make your experience more rewarding.

8. Go Gentle on Yourself: If you miss a day, go gentle on yourself. You can pick up reading tomorrow. Grace is at the heart of our relationship with Jesus.

The Bible Reading Plan

See the Bible Reading Plan at GrahamJosephHill/BibleReading-Plan. This will be updated as each book of the Bible is completed for the devotional books and podcast.

Appendix 3

Other Books and Resources by Graham Joseph Hill

Author and Ministry Websites

Linktr.ee/dailydevotions

GrahamJosephHill.com

TheGlobalChurchProject.com

Books

Healing Our Broken Humanity: Practices for Revitalizing the Church and Renewing the World. Downers Grove, IL: InterVarsity, 2018 (with Grace Ji-Sun Kim).

Hide This in Your Heart: Memorizing Scripture for Kingdom Impact. Colorado Springs, CO: NavPress, 2020 (with Michael Frost).

Holding Up Half the Sky: A Biblical Case for Women Leading and Teaching in the Church. Eugene, OR: Cascade, 2020.

Salt, Light, and a City, Second Edition: Conformation—Ecclesiology for the Global Missional Community: Volume 2, Majority World Voices. Eugene, OR: Cascade, 2020.

Salt, Light, and a City, Second Edition: Ecclesiology for the Global Missional Community: Volume 1, Western Voices. Eugene, OR: Cascade, 2017.

The Soul Online: Bereavement, Social Media, and Competent Care. Eugene, OR: Wipf and Stock, 2022 (with Desiree Geldenhuys).

Sunburnt Country, Sweeping Pains: The Experiences of Asian Australian Women in Ministry and Mission. Eugene, OR: Wipf and Stock, 2022.

World Christianity: An Introduction. Eugene, OR: Cascade, 2024.